The West Coast
GOES TO WAR
1941–1942

BY Don DeNevi

PICTORIAL HISTORIES PUBLISHING COMPANY, INC.
Missoula, Montana

Copyright © 1998 by Don DeNevi

All rights reserved. No portion of this book may be
used or reproduced without permission of the publisher.

Library of Congress
Catalog Card No. 98-66198

ISBN 1-57510-038-X

FIRST PRINTING March 1998

EDITING Carol Van Valkenburg
TYPOGRAPHY Arrow Graphics
LAYOUT Stan Cohen
COVER GRAPHICS Mike Egeler

PICTORIAL HISTORIES PUBLISHING COMPANY, INC.
713 South Third Street West
Missoula, Montana 59801

PREFACE

On Dec. 7, 1941, the Japanese attack on the United States Naval Base at Pearl Harbor in the Hawaiian Islands signaled the real beginning of World War II for the United States. The attack's devastating blow to the U.S. Navy removed a significant bastion of defense for the people living on the West Coast. During the year preceding the attack, the United States and the Japanese governments had become increasingly distant. The Japanese were involved in a war with China and were steadily increasing their role in Southeast Asia. As the end of 1941 approached, relations between the two countries deteriorated at a quick pace. The War in Europe was raging and, because of United States ties with Britain and France, it had diplomatic priority. Although the United States monitored the Japanese situation, it did not seem to be of major importance. Nonetheless much effort went into preparing the country, and particularly the West Coast, for the inevitability of war.

After the attack on Pearl Harbor, the West Coast was extremely vulnerable to a land invasion force and bombing attacks. From Dec. 7 on, the people on the West Coast were confronted not only with the fact that the country was at war with Japan, Germany and Italy, but also with preparations for the possibility of an enemy force invading their shores and bombing their cities. Although there was a great deal of preparation prior to the Pearl Harbor attack, the realization that the threat was now very real created changes in the lives of everyone on the coast. Recording the impact of those events on the people of the West Coast is the purpose of this book.

Radio, newspapers, and the telephone were the basic methods of mass communication in 1941 and the major sources of information about the war. Some of what Americans learned was correct, some was exaggerated, some was false and much was plain rumor. But it was this information, true or false, that led to decisions and action.

Historically, situations that grow out of fear and uncertainty bring out a high level of patriotism and sometimes result in acts that violate Constitutional rights and freedoms. So it was in those days and hindsight can find many such breaches. But those who faced the threats did not see their actions as improper. This is not to justify their response, for history has a grand way of making its own judgments from the valued position of time. Their actions do reveal how information from newspapers, statesmen, and military authorities, coupled with historical precedence, created an atmosphere in which certain events happened.

We have tried not to make value judgments. The people who lived through the events have their own.

The scope of this book is necessarily limited to the three states comprising the continental western boundary of the United States.

The threat of enemy invasion or bombing attacks remained imminent through the first half of 1942 and marshalled a tremendous amount of patriotism and human sacrifice. It also made people prepare their homes and businesses against an attack they were told was sure to come. Then in mid-1942, the United States Navy scored a stunning victory in the Battle of Midway and the naval balance of power shifted to the United States. This event all but removed the threat of an enemy invasion and even mitigated the possibility of a bombing attack. It did not, however, remove the fear of saboteurs and enemy agents and precautions against them continued for the war's duration. It did allow West Coast residents to relax somewhat and devote full concentration to their part in building an unparalleled war machine.

It has been more than 50 years since all this happened. For many Americans it is only a part of a history book. For those who then lived on the West Coast, it is vivid memories of events unmatched in our short history.

—Don DeNevi

INTRODUCTION

Early on the morning of June 3, 1942, nearly six months after the debacle of Pearl Harbor, American and Japanese naval forces clashed in what was to become one of the most decisive naval engagements of the Second World War. The battle was joined near Midway, a tiny island in the Central Pacific, 1,500 miles from Hawaii. By the afternoon of June 5, four aircraft carriers of the Japanese fleet commanded by Admiral Isoruku Yamamoto had either been sunk or heavily damaged by the American naval and army air forces of Admiral Chester W. Nimitz.

The Japanese fleet retired, and Midway Island remained firmly in American hands. If Imperial Japan had ever hoped to invade the continental United States by attacking the Pacific Coast, those hopes were dashed at Midway.

The people living on America's West Coast could now breathe a collective sigh of relief. Since the Japanese attack on Pearl Harbor and the devastation of the American fleet, the Pacific Coast had lived under the threat—sometimes real, sometimes only perceived—of land invasion or aerial bombardment. Pearl Harbor and the Battle of Midway bracketed six months of courage, sacrifice, and resolution, sadly blemished by the racism and xenophobia that resulted in Executive Order 9066 and the internment of Japanese Americans.

Certainly the months from Pearl Harbor to Midway were unparalleled in American History. No invader, after all, had either threatened or stepped on the soil of the continental United States since the War of 1812. Two vast oceans insulated our shores from European and Asian bellicosity. But after Pearl Harbor that insularity was lost forever. A tiny Asian island nation, only recently industrialized, and located thousands of sea miles from America had attacked and severely crippled the ships of our Pacific fleet, the West Coast's first line of defense. And Japan had done so with apparent ease, expertise, and impunity. By the time the antiaircraft guns at Pearl Harbor had cooled, America and the West Coast realized that the war we dreaded yet suspected would come would be long and bloody and waged against an adversary far stronger than we thought.

Certain it was that we were strong, that we would recover, re-arm, and recoup our losses. But behind the rallying slogan of "Remember Pearl Harbor" and the foolish bravado of such songs as "You're a Sap, Mr. Jap" was the vague unease, strongly felt on the Pacific Coast, that this war would touch us all.

On the West Coast, vague unease—and doubt and fear—entered the most mundane of citizens' everyday activities. If the Japanese could attack Hawaii, what might their next target be? The sprawling aircraft plants in Seattle and Los Angeles? The huge military installations in San Diego, San Francisco and Oakland? Would fifth columnists blow up the Golden Gate Bridge or poison the miles of aqueducts supplying water to Southern California?

That, of course, never happened.

No Japanese planes ever threatened the West Coast. No Axis saboteurs were ever found. Most people know this through the clarity of hindsight. Some suspected as much as early as the last few weeks of December 1941.

Ironically, the Axis threat to the West Coast—indeed, to the rest of the nation as well—was so remote by mid-1942 that the newly formed Office of War Information worried that America's national resolve would crumble. Even more ironic, the menace of attack or sabotage on the West Coast was generated not by any of the enemy's strategic goals but by a cynical, heavy-handed manipulation of Americans' deepest fears and hazy, self-righteous notions of patriotism. Americans were more afraid of an enemy crudely—and often racially—caricatured in a defense-plant poster than of the enemy himself.

But ignorance, if it is not bliss, can surely become fear as it did on the West Coast in the first six months of the war. Not privy to information concerning the Japanese strategy, people were uneasy, afraid; many, as we shall see, were downright petrified. Because from Pearl Harbor to Midway, the West Coast just didn't know.

It is the story of those six months that we have attempted to tell in *The West Coast Goes to War*. Our narrative has been enhanced tremendously by the availability of the accompanying photographs, many of which have not been published since 1942 and which tell the story far more eloquently, clearly and convincingly than names and dates ever could. Pearl Harbor to Midway was an unprecedented time on America's West Coast, the beginning of a change still being felt. Our account, we hope, is a long-needed chronicle and recollection.

ACKNOWLEDGMENTS

West Coast Goes to War was prepared with the help of a remarkable group of individuals. Their commitment to having the story told as well as their thorough search for the most relevant photographs, made the book possible. Their exhaustive help is genuinely appreciated, for they are the real authors.

They are: Roy Grimm, Managing Editor of the *Oakland Tribune*; Yae Shinomiya, Assistant Librarian of the *Oakland Tribune*; Sue Lenmon, Historian of the Mare Island Shipyard; John Shackleton, Public Affairs Officer at the U.S. Naval Air Station, Moffett Field; Retired United States Coast Guard officers Captain R. Ridgely, Vice Admiral D. McG. Morrison, Admiral C.R. Bender, and Captain R.R. Smith; Marilyn Phipps, Historical Services, the Boeing Company; Don Barncoli and Mary Phillips, Archivists, Kaiser Industries; Norman Anthony, researcher, U.S. General Services Administration Archives, San Bruno, Calif.; George Grosskopf, Director, Public Relations, 12th Coast Guard District, P.A.O. San Francisco; Nancy Pitt, Administrative Assistant, Port of San Francisco Commission; Karl Kortum, Director, San Francisco Maritime Museum; Howard Thomas, Director of Public Relations, U.S. Naval Air Station, Alameda, Calif.; John Maounis, Researcher Archivist, San Francisco Maritime Museum; James Dernan, Curator, Photographic Division, Oakland Museum; Warren Miller, Director, Railway Negative Exchange; Elsie Flanagan, Researcher, California Historical Society; Brian Geary, Director, Public Relations, Bechtel Corporation; Captain E.J. Scheyser, USN Commander, Mare Island Naval Shipyard; Steve Harding, Director, U.S. Naval Marine Museum, Treasure Island; Gladys Hansen, Director, San Francisco Room, San Francisco Public Library; Eric Saul, Director, Public Relations, Bethlehem Shipyards; Demitra Georgas, Bancroft Library, University of California, Berkeley; John Shepard, General Manager, AAA Shipyards, Hunters Point; Anna Krayton, Archivist, *San Francisco Chronicle*; John Schumate, Director, Public Relations, American Association of Railroads; Mrs. Isabel Green and Mrs. Eileen De Stefand, Archivists, Still Photo Division, Pentagon; Bob Shina, Coast Guard Historian, U.S. Coast Guard, Washington, D.C.; Mrs. Eleanor Hoover, Archivist, Naval History Center, Washington, D.C.; Beverly Brannan, Prints and Photograph Division, Library of Congress, Washington, D.C., and John Coldwell, Library of Congress, Washington, D.C.

Special thanks to Frank Bartholomew, Murray Bolen, Glenville Taylor, Frank Tremaine and Sandra Uenten.

DEDICATION

AS A TOKEN of friendship, to say nothing of my highest respect and admiration, I dedicate this book to Kazuo Masai, the best friend a growing boy could have, and to my other Nisei friends at Edison High School in Stockton, California, during the early 1950s. Those include Joan Nakawatase, Lester Matsune, Ken Nishikawa, Robert Yasui, Yoshiaki Murano, and many, many others.

To the Nishimoto brothers, Cyrus, Dan, Victor, Edgar, and Lloyd, I will never forget that late afternoon in 1946 when you and the family arrived home on Commerce Street after a week of traveling from that barren, isolated mountain-desert internment camp. Without a word to those of us kids who had anticipated your arrival, you slowly walked up to your old home and started pulling off the boards that had protected the doors and windows for four years. Later, deeply human and so full of kindness and gentleness, you became a life-long inspiration to me.

All of you are a part of me.

—DON DENEVI

CONTENTS

Chapter One   *1*
PRE-WAR VIEWS

Chapter Two   *13*
WHERE'S PEARL HARBOR?

Chapter Three   *17*
A STATE OF EMERGENCY

Chapter Four   *55*
RAINBOW 5

Chapter Five   *59*
FEAR, RACISM AND SADNESS

Chapter Six   *79*
THE WEST COAST ROLLS UP ITS SLEEVES

Chapter Seven   *101*
SHANGRI-LA AND MIDWAY:
THE END OF THE BEGINNING

Chapter Eight   *113*
A PHOTO POTPOURRI

Chapter Nine   *121*
LEGACY OF THE WAR

Bibliography & About the Author   *130*

All photos are from the Pictorial Histories Publishing Company collection unless otherwise noted.
FDR Library—Hyde Park, NY
LC—Library of Congress, Washington, D.C.

CHAPTER ONE
Pre-War Views

TOP PHOTO: In August 1933 Emperor Hirohito reviewed the Japanese fleet off Yokohama. The ceremony ended the grand maneuvers of the fleet, which lasted three months and covered most of the western Pacific Ocean. The photo was taken from the stern of the Emperor's flagship, the converted battle cruiser *Niysi*, as it steamed between long lines of warships, 161 in all, totalling 850,000 tons. The new 10,000-ton cruiser *Atago* follows the *Niysi*. BOTTOM PHOTO: The *Tatsuta Maru* sails under the Golden Gate Bridge on July 30, 1941, making port after she had lurked off the coast for six days, uncertain of her reception by the U.S. government authorities.

Scenes such as this greeted residents of the central California coast in January 1940 as the defending "blue" army awaited attack by "black" army to start war games. The army was actually totally mechanized by this time.

Maneuvers of the 757th Tank Battalion at Fort Ord in November 1941.

Two 14-inch railway guns were assembled into a special train at Fort MacArthur in June 1938. They were taken south of San Clemente to allow soldiers to practice firing at a moving target that simulated a battleship, 20 miles at sea. This was the first time in eight years that the guns were fired.

Douglas SBD "Dauntless" torpedo bombers in practice formation from their base at North Island, San Diego, in March 1940. The plane was considered one of the best carrier-based aircraft that the U.S. Navy put in action during the war.

A lineup of Vultee BT-13 "Valiant" army training planes at the Vultee plant in Los Angeles. This popular trainer was built from 1940 to 1944. It was used by the army in basic flight training throughout the war.

This Ocober 1941 photo shows a security guard detachment at Hamilton Field armed with the latest weapon, Thompson submachine guns. They are guarding the P-40 fighters, based at the field, against attack by parachute troops.

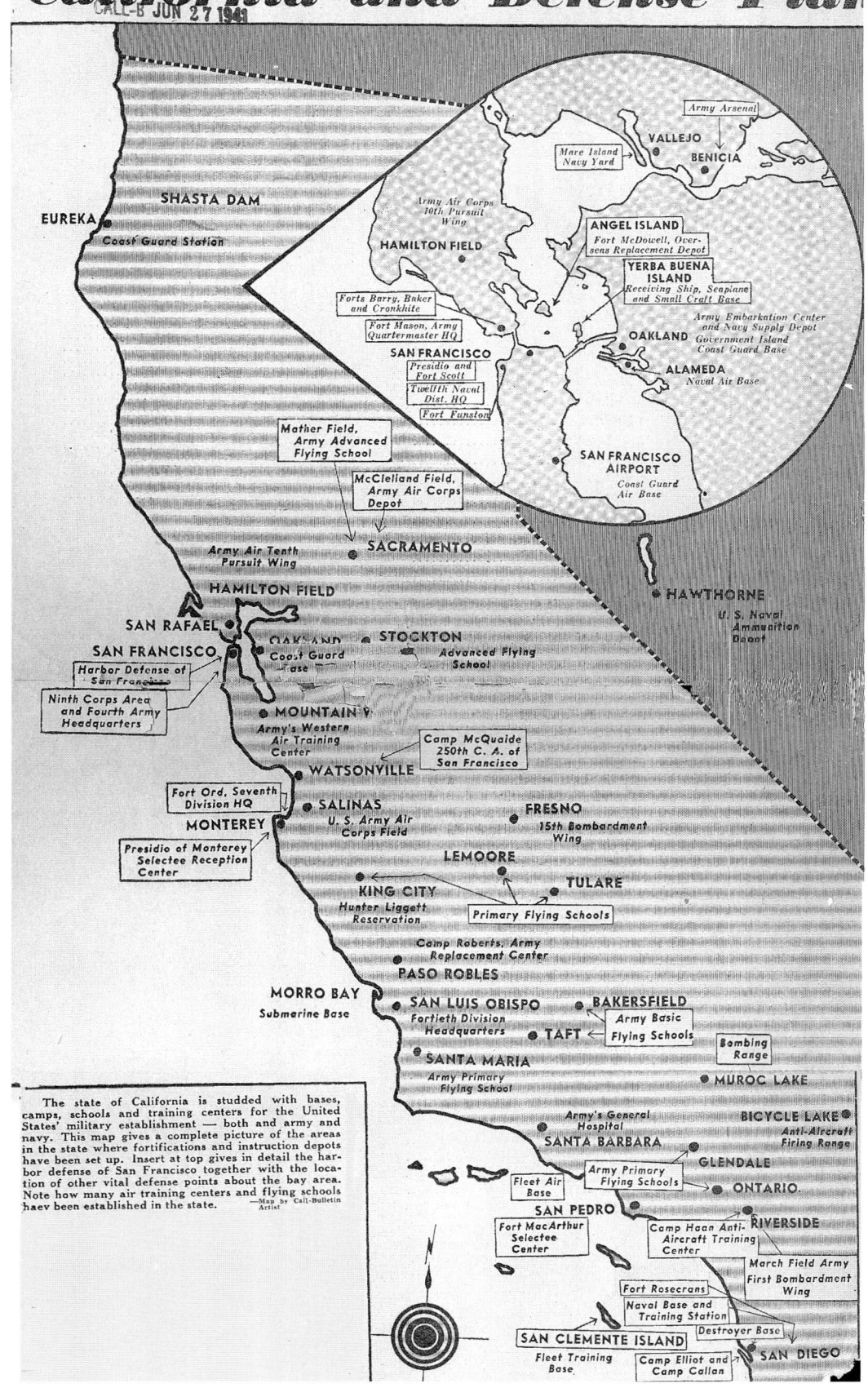

A group of Tacoma, Washington, men in training as "Home Guards," armed with rifles, shotguns and World War One "tin hats," November 1940.

ABOVE INSET: Barracks at Camp Roberts, near Paso Robles, California, in April 1941. It was a major army replacement center.

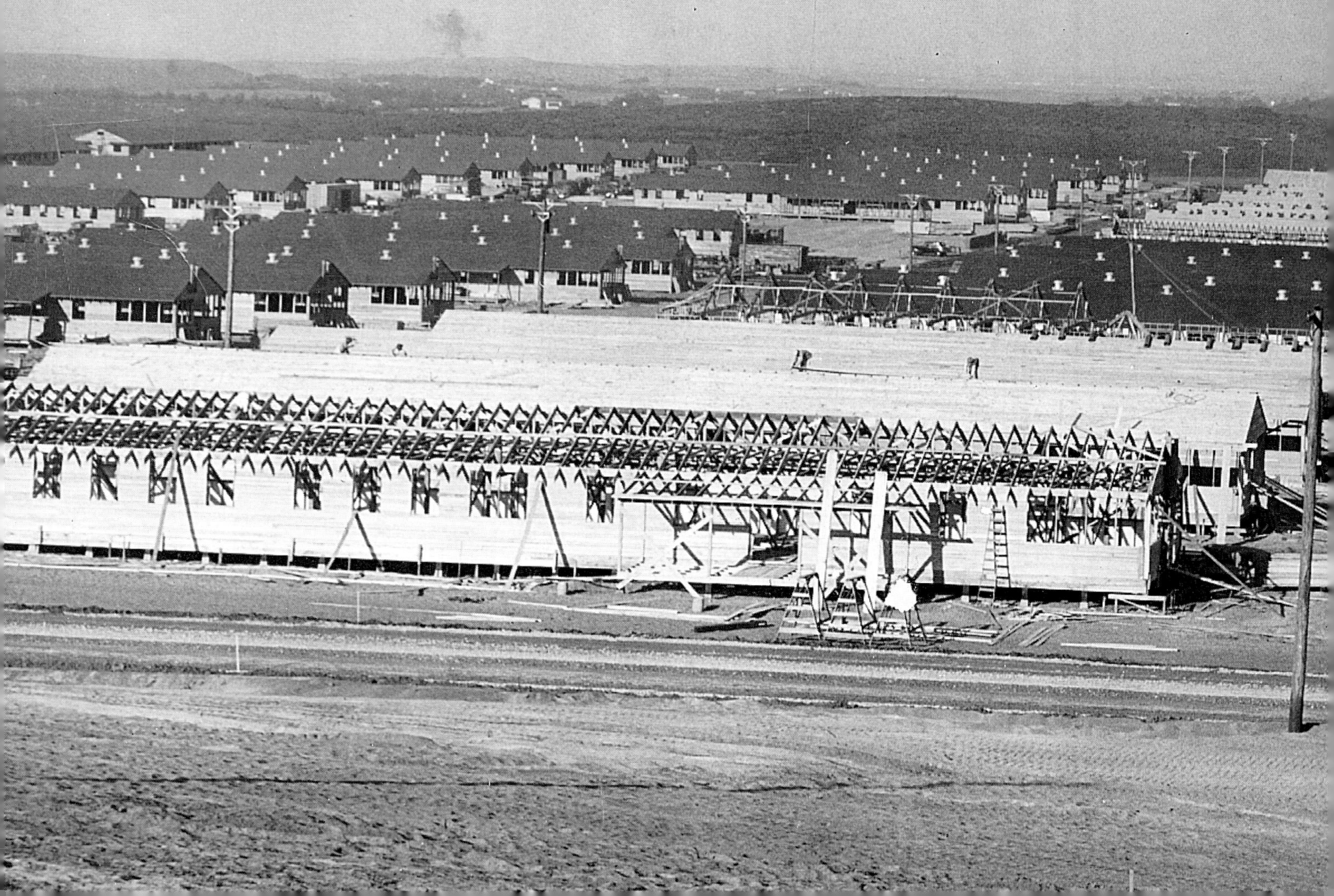

Fort Ord, near Monterey, California, was a major army traning base and headquarters for the Seventh Division.

The press release for this famous photo reads as follows: *"Wings Of The Navy"* Here is the first photograph ever made of the U.S. Naval Air Base at North Island, near San Diego, Calif., with its full complement of PBY2's, the most powerful and efficient air armada of any navy in the world. Seven squadrons (twelve planes to a squadron) of these facile, deadly sentinels of the sky were based at this concrete-covered, man-made island during the shooting of Warner Bros. saga of naval aviation, "Wings Of The Navy" (preparations for a "take" are visible in the foreground). Statistics on these "big boats" (Navy slang): length—63½ ft.; height—18½ ft.; wing-spread—105 ft. They have a cruising radius of 3500 miles, weigh 14 tons with a full seven-man crew and battle load. The 44 planes shown in this rare photograph had just arrived at their home station after a mass formation, non-stop flight from Seattle, where they refueled after patrolling and surveying Alaskan waters. Seventeen of the assembled ships took off just after this photo was made and winged their way, in perfect formation, to Honolulu—a "routine" assignment for these craft that fly so casually over seas and continents without stop. They're America's safeguard—these "Wings Of The Navy." From: Warner Bros. Studio, Burbank, California, 1939.

Aerial view of the U.S. Naval Air Station in Alameda, California, in October 1940. It shows seaplane hangars, lagoons, barracks, administration building, plane assembly and repair shops and other structures. Beyond these buildings can be seen the runways and hangars of the San Francisco Bay Airdrome.
CLYDE H. SUNDERLAND PHOTO

A sign of the times in early 1941. This sign was at the Southern Pacific Railroad yard in the Bay area. Defense jobs were plentiful up and down the West Coast in the early 1940s.

CHAPTER TWO

Where's Pearl Harbor?

THE WEST COAST went to war shortly after 10:30 A.M., Pacific Standard Time on Dec. 7, 1941. It was then that James Sullivan, the weekend bureau manager for United Press International in San Francisco received the first of a startling series of urgent cables sent from Honolulu.

In Hawaii, shortly after 8:00 A.M., Frank Tremaine, UPI's Honolulu bureau chief, awoke to the deep-throated roar of radial aircraft engines, punctuated by the crack of antiaircraft fire and exploding bombs. Tremaine's home commanded a view of Pearl Harbor. He could see Battleship Row from his bedroom window. It was from there that he telephoned his first terse message over the wires of the Commercial Cable Co. to Sullivan on the California mainland: Unidentified Aircraft Attacking Pearl HarborxTremainexMore.[1] Tremaine's second cable identified the enemy aircraft: They bore the "meatball" insigne of the Japanese Navy.

Sullivan was stunned. Anybody who had read a newspaper, listened to the radio, or watched a Pathe newsreel in the last three years suspected Japan would eventually attack the United States. But so close to home? At a naval bastion so secure as Pearl Harbor, for Chrissakes? It gave Sullivan, the seasoned newsman, a moment's pause. Then he flagged Tremaine's dispatches "flash" and began transcribing them to New York and the rest of the nation over UPI's national trunk lines.

Then we all knew—or soon would. At 11:00 A.M., from KIRO in Seattle to KFSD in San Diego, most West Coast radio stations were broadcasting local programs, with the barest of Sunday morning crews. Only in Los Angeles, at the National Broadcasting Company studios at Sunset and Vine in Hollywood, was there much activity. The casts of the Jack Benny and Burns and Allen shows were rehearsing for late afternoon broadcasts to the East Coast. In San Francisco, station KGO's "Great Plays" program had just begun the first act of Gogol's *The Inspector General*; in Los Angeles, station KFOX featured a program of recorded swing music.

Shortly after 11:00 the Mutual, CBS, and NBC Blue and Red networks interrupted local programming on the Pacific Coast with one- or two-sentence announce-

Scrap metal stored at Portland, Oregon, bound for Japan, 1940.

ments of what James Sullivan had been the first on the West Coast to know: The United States had been attacked by Japan, and very close to our shores.

First reactions to the electrifying news broadcasts ranged from shock to anger and disbelief. Even more reactions registered downright puzzlement, for few on the West Coast were familiar with the acute deterioration of Japanese and American diplomacy that had launched Admiral Nagumo's airplanes against Pearl Harbor. Who? The Japs? Why them? Why would they attack us? Easily the most common question that morning was asked by Margaret Ensign, who heard the news in her Los Angeles apartment: "We were listening to the radio. We had been out late in Hollywood the night before and were having a late breakfast sometime around 11:00 or so. There was a musical program on the radio, and the announcer broke in and said that the Navy had been bombed at Pearl Harbor. At first we thought it was the Invasion from Mars hoax all over again. When the second announcement came, Dick [her husband] and I looked at each other and said, 'Where's Pearl Harbor?'"

---

1. Tremaine and UPI had the scoop of the decade. In 1941, news dispatches reached the mainland only one way: by telegraph through the office of the Commercial Cable Co. in downtown Honolulu. Commercial Cable had but one outside telephone line, and Tremaine, being the first to call in, could thus hold the line open. "Nobody else could call a story in [to be then cabled to the mainland]," Tremaine recalled years later. "I got the first call in and put my wife, Kay, on the line to keep it open. She'd read the dispatches to Commercial as I shouted them to her from the window. We sat on that line until 9:00 or so. Then I gave the other boys a chance." (Frank Tremaine, personal communication, 1982.)

Result of the Pearl Harbor attack. The destroyers *Cassin* and *Downes* with the battleship *Pennsylvania*. The battleship *Arizona* is burning in the background. USN

EXTRA

San Francisco Examiner

VOL. CLXXV, NO. 161 — SAN FRANCISCO, MONDAY, DECEMBER 8, 1941—28 PAGES — DAILY 5 CENTS, SUNDAY 10 CENTS

U.S.-JAP WAR!

HAWAII, MANILA BOMBED; TWO U. S. WARSHIPS SUNK

President Announces Attacks

WASHINGTON, Dec. 7.—(INS)—President Roosevelt issued the following statement at 2:25 p. m. through Secretary Stephen T Early:

"The Japanese have attacked Pearl Harbor from the air and all naval and military activities on the island of Oahu, the principal American base in the Hawaiian Islands.

Twenty minutes after announcing officially that the Japanese air force had attacked American naval bases in Hawaii, the White House announced the Japanese also attacked Manila.

The announcement of the attack on Manila read:

"A second attack is reported. This one has been made on the American and naval station in Manila."

S. F. Defenses on War Basis; Leaves Cancelled

San Francisco's defenses swung into action within minutes of the Japanese attack on Manila and Honolulu yesterday.

The Navy, Army and Coast Guard cancelled all leaves, rounded up every man and sent them to battle stations.

Agents began streaming into offices of the Federal Bureau of Investigation, apparently to receive final orders preparatory to a roundup of all suspected spies and dangerous aliens.

All San Francisco police of all details were ordered to report, apparently to participate in the roundup.

There was intense activity at Fourth Army headquarters, where Lieut. Gen. John L. DeWitt, top Army officer of the Pacific coast as Fourth Army commander, was closeted throughout the afternoon with his staff.

Busier still was the office of Rear Admiral John W. Greenslade, who as commandant of the Twelfth Naval District is in charge of San Francisco's defense at sea.

Great Navy patrol bombers swept up and down the California co ast off the Golden Gate on a ceaseless patrol. Vessels of the Navy Patrol Force operating from Treasure Island were sent to stations at sea in vastly increased numbers.

ALL SHIPS HALTED.

All marine operations in San Francisco Bay except those of the Navy were brought to a halt.

Full crews manned every one of the eight to sixteen inch rifles that from seaward from both sides of the Golden Gate.

Brig. Gen. E. A. Stockton, commanding harbor defenses, published at once an order cancelling all leaves and furloughs.

San Francisco police responded at once to requests from the Army and Navy and began stopping all soldiers and sailors on downtown streets to order them to report to their stations.

There still was no police guard at the Japanese consulate late in the afternoon.

Yoshio Muto, the Japanese consul, appeared stunned.

"I don't understand! I don't understand!" he kept repeating. San Francisco outwardly maintained its customary Sunday quiet.

$700,000 Granted Monterey Airport

MONTEREY, Dec. 6—(AP)—Word was received today that President Roosevelt has authorized a $700,000 improvement project for the Monterey airport.

Runways will be extended and paved, the field will be lighted, and extensive grading and re alignment will be done. The WPA will do the work. A $250,000 bond issue will be authorized by the district board to cover the sponsor's share of the cost.

WASHINGTON, Dec. 7.—(INS) — President Roosevelt has ordered the Army and Navy to use their full power for the defense of the United States.

"As soon as word of the attack was taken to the President," Early said, "The President directed the Army and Navy to execute all previously prepared plans for defense of the United States."

War Secretary Stimson and Navy Secretary Knox immediately conferred with the President at the White House.

The White House revealed that the attacks by Japan were made "wholly without warning."

Steps immediately were taken by the White House to notify congressional leaders of the grave situation.

WASHINGTON, Dec. 7. — (AP) — The President decided today after Japan's attack on Pearl Harbor and Manila to call an extraordinarily meeting of the Cabinet for 8:30 p. m. tonight and to have congressional leaders of both parties join the conference at 9 p. m.

NEW YORK, Dec. 7.—(AP)—Untold damage has been done to the United States Naval Base at Pearl Harbor and to the city of Honolulu itself by unidentified bombing planes, an NBC observer reported today in a broadcast direct from Honolulu.

The observer, standing on the roof of the Advertiser Building in Honolulu, said the planes, undoubtedly Japanese, made the raid unexpectedly. His report was suddenly broken off.

BULLETINS

MANILA, Dec. 7.—(INS)—The American naval base at Cavite, Island of Luzon, was subjected to enemy attack this morning.

Army and Navy authorities commanded all forces to their stations to resist the attack.

There were no immediate reports on damage.

HONOLULU, Dec. 7. — (INS) — The United States Army issued an official statement this morning declaring enemy aircraft have been shot down.

WASHINGTON, Dec. 7.—(INS)—Senate leaders were preparing today for an emergency session tomorrow in anticipation of a message from President Roosevelt asking for a declaration of war against Japan.

SAN PEDRO, Dec. 7.—(INS)—Every naval officer and mechanician attached to the San Pedro air base was ordered by broadcast today to report immediately to his station.

WASHINGTON, Dec. 7.—(INS)—The White House said at 3:30 p. m., that the Japanese attacks upon Hawaii and the Philippines apparently were still in progress at that time.

First news of the attacks was received by the War and Navy Departments, and it was instantly transmitted to President Roosevelt.

There was deep amazement as well as resentment in officialdom over the attacks while the United States and Japan were still holding conferences in an effort to maintain peace.

Even as Japan's envoys were professing that they were trying to find a peaceful solution of the Far East situation the attacks were launched.

WASHINGTON, Dec. 7.—(INS)—The War Department announced that an American transport has been torpedoed 1,300 miles west of San Francisco.

WASHINGTON, Dec. 7.—(INS)—Presidential Secretary Stephen T. Early announced at 3:35 p. m. that the Army has received distress signals from a vessel believed to be one of its cargo ships 700 miles off San Francisco. It was not immediately known if this ship might have been the same one referred to shortly before in an announcement by the War Department, or whether it constituted a second attack.

Severe Explosions Rock Pearl Harbor In Surprise Attack

HONOLULU, Dec. 7.—(AP)—Japanese bombs killed at least five persons and injured many others, three seriously, in a surprise morning aerial attack on Honolulu today.

HONOLULU, Dec. 7.—(INS)—America's outpost of the Pacific, mighty Pearl Harbor naval base was under enemy attack today.

A number of attacking planes, with red insignia were sighted shortly after 8 a. m.

(In Washington Presidential Secretary Early identified the attacking planes as Japanese.)

Antiaircraft guns opened fire when the planes dived low over the base and released repeated sticks of bombs.

Two Warships Sunk

Two warships lying in the harbor were sunk.

The planes later returned to the attack.

The attack was a complete surprise with minimum forces of the Army and Navy on Sunday morning duty.

A pall of heavy black smoke hung over Pearl Harbor.

Sporadic Air Raids

Army Intelligence said:

"Pearl Harbor was subjected to a sporadic air raid. We have no further details."

Antiaircraft guns are still firing from positions near the center of Honolulu.

United States Army fighter planes have taken to the air.

A round of explosions of great magnitude were heard at 9:30 a. m., more than an hour after the first raid.

A Redding, California, newsboy sells newspapers on Dec. 7, 1941. LC-USF34-71206-D

CHAPTER THREE

A State of Emergency

SUDDENLY, THE Pacific Coast faced a tremendous challenge. Soon after word of the attack spread, residents rushed to complete measures for defense, and civilian defense officials and volunteers quickly moved to a war footing. Air-raid sirens were mustered out and tested. In the Bay Area, factory whistles and fire house sirens were readied as the principal means of alarm. Defense councils worked through the night of Dec. 7, locked behind courthouse doors. They drew up plans to extinguish all lights upon warning, especially advertising signs. Vital areas had to be protected against sabotage and attack.

In Los Angeles, the Board of Supervisors immediately placed the county in a state of emergency. This action followed a meeting late Sunday of all the state and county defense councils, which at the same time ordered tests of the air raid defenses in a blackout in the harbor areas. The first reaction of the Los Angeles citizens to the Japanese attack was a rush to enlist in military and civilian defense organizations. Applicants for the Navy, Marines, Coast Guard and Army clogged the city's recruiting offices, while thousands of men and women volunteered for such civilian defense jobs as air watchers and military canteen workers. In San Quentin prison, 10 convicts on death row volunteered to fight the enemy by becoming, somehow, "human torpedoes." No one, it seemed, wanted to be left out of the national effort.

The commandant of the Eleventh Naval District advised blacking out San Diego. By Monday night a protective blackout was ordered over a 15-mile radius not only in San Diego but also in Los Angeles, from the Port of San Pedro to Fort MacArthur. Women and children were requested to leave such obviously strategic areas as harbors, oil fields, and neighborhoods near airplane factories. More than 200 Army wives and children were evacuated from Fort MacArthur. From Sunday on, military restrictions barred the public from the fort and other strategic areas such as Terminal Island, the Long Beach and Signal Hill oil fields, and the airplane factories in Burbank and Inglewood.

Following a blackout of the Lockheed and Mines Field airports, the Civil Aeronautics Authority cancelled all commercial airline flights arriving and departing Los Angeles. The Vultee and North American aircraft factories in Inglewood were blacked out for the night; evening shifts were sent home and graveyard shifts were instructed not to report to work. Douglas Aircraft reported a brief blackout of its Santa Monica plant but later said that several graveyard shifts at all three of its factories, including El Segundo and the large new plant in Long Beach, would continue normal operations. The Lockheed, Vega and Northrup aircraft companies were working normal shifts.

Armed guards patrolled the Los Angeles-Long Beach harbors. By Sunday evening, the patrols included Terminal Island's wharves, warehouses and shipyards, as well as the Wilmington oil fields and storage facilities. The harbor was closed to all shipping.

By mid-morning of Dec. 8, little more than 24 hours since the Japanese attack, banner headlines in extra additions of West Coast newspapers announced the U.S. declaration of war with Japan. At 9:30 A.M. Pacific time, people on the West Coast had turned on their radios to hear President Roosevelt address a joint session of Congress, opening his 10-minute speech with the historic "Yesterday, Dec. 7, 1941—a date which will live in infamy—the United States of America was suddenly and deliberately attacked by naval and air forces of the Empire of Japan." Thunderous applause greeted the conclusion of Roosevelt's address; his joint resolution asking for war was approved nearly unanimously by both houses of Congress.[1]

The President's speech roused a whole nation; it was a call to arms and an appeal for national unity and patriotism. The President spoke of "confidence in our armed forces" and "the unbounded determination of our people . . . to gain the inevitable triumph." But for those on the West Coast, the President's message was a

---
1. Congresswoman Jeannette Rankin of Montana cast the lone "nay" vote. She had also voted against war with Germany in 1917.

EXTRA

Los Angeles Times

VOL. LXI — Three Parts — 38 Pages — ★★★ — MONDAY MORNING, DECEMBER 8, 1941. — Page A — DAILY, FIVE CENTS

IT'S WAR!

Hostilities Declared by Japanese; 350 Reported Killed in Hawaii Raid

U.S. Battleships Hit; 7 Die in Honolulu

NEW YORK, Dec. 7. (A.P.)—Three hundred and fifty men were killed by a direct bomb hit on Hickam Field, an N.B.C. observer reported tonight from Honolulu.

In addition to these casualties from an air raid by planes which the observer identified as Japanese, he said three United States ships, including the battleship Oklahoma, were attacked in Pearl Harbor.

Several of the attacking planes, which came from the south, were shot down, he said.

HONOLULU, Dec. 7. (A.P.)—Japanese bombs killed at least seven persons and injured many others, three seriously, in a surprise morning aerial attack on Honolulu today.

Army officials announced that two Japanese planes had been shot down in the Honolulu area.

The dead included three Caucasians, two Japanese and a 10-year-old Portuguese girl.

Several fires were started in the city area, but all were immediately controlled.

Governor Joseph B. Poindexter proclaimed M-Day emergency defense measures immediately in effect. He appointed Eduard Doty in charge of the Major Disaster Council.

The M-Day proclamation establishes civilian-military control of traffic and roads, and permits the Governor to issue food ration regulations.

First reports said that 10 or more persons were injured when enemy planes sprayed bullets on the streets of Wahiawa, a town of about 3000 population, about 20 miles northwest of Honolulu.

This report indicated the aerial attack was aimed at points on the island of Oahu other than Honolulu and the heavily fortified Pearl Harbor naval base.

The attack ended at around 9:25 a.m., (11:55 a.m. P.S.T.) lasting for ap

Turn to Page B, Column 7

LATE WAR BULLETINS

SHANGHAI, Dec. 8 (Monday.) (A.P.)—The Japanese have sunk the British gunboat Petrel as it lay off the International Settlement waterfront.

HONOLULU, Dec. 7. (U.P.) — Parachute troops were sighted off Pearl Harbor today.

TOKYO, Dec. 8 (Monday.) (A.P.)—An emergency session of the Japanese Cabinet was held at Premier Tojo's official residence at 7 a.m. today (2 p.m. Sunday, P.S.T.)

NEW YORK, Dec. 7. (U.P.)—The U.S.S. Oklahoma, a battleship, was set afire in today's air attack on Pearl Harbor, an N.B.C. broadcast from Honolulu said.

WASHINGTON, Dec. 7. (A.P.)—The Navy Department announced tonight that a censorship had been placed on all outgoing cablegrams and radio messages from the United States and its outlying possessions.

LONDON, Dec. 7. (P)—The House of Commons was summoned tonight for a session tomorrow.

The House of Lords also was called.

An announcement from Prime Minister

Turn to Page B, Column 3

Air Guards, Attention!

To chief observers: All observation posts: A.W.S. (Aircraft Warning Service) You are directed to activate your observation posts immediately and to see that the post is fully manned at all times.

By order Brig. Gen. William O. Ryan, Commander, Ft. Interceptor Command.

Air Bombs Rained on Pacific Bases

WASHINGTON, Dec. 7. (A.P.)—The White House announced early tonight that the Navy had advised the President that Japan has attacked the island of Guam.

WASHINGTON, Dec. 7. (A.P.)—Japan declared war upon the United States today. An electrified nation immediately united for a terrific struggle ahead. President Roosevelt was expected to ask Congress for a declaration of war tomorrow.

During the day, Japanese planes bombed Manila, Honolulu, Pearl Harbor, and Hickam Field, Hawaii, without warning. In a broadcast from Honolulu, some 350 soldiers were reported dead at Hickam Field, with numerous casualties at the other points of attack. (The attack on Manila was announced by the White House. The Associated Press correspondent there reported at 1:25 p.m. (P.S.T.) that Manila was quiet.) President Roosevelt said he hoped the report of the bombing of the Philippine capital "at least is erroneous."

Then, the Tokyo government announced that Japan had entered a state of war with the United States and Great Britain as of 6 a.m., tomorrow (1 p.m. P.S.T. Sunday.)

But President Roosevelt hardly waited for the Japanese declaration. As soon as he heard of the bombing he ordered the Army and Navy to carry out previously prepared and highly secret plans for the defense of the country.

Army airmen engaged Japanese fighting planes over Honolulu. In the city below them, the White House said, a heavy loss of life had been inflicted, together with extensive damage to property.

At the same time, the Chief Executive called his Cabinet into extraordinary session for 8:30 p.m., and invited Congressional leaders to join the group a half-hour later.

Prior to this meeting, Mr. Roosevelt began the draft of a special message to Congress and if the general sentiment in official Washington quarters was any indication, Japan's declaration of war would be met in like terms by the Commander-in-Chief.

From a high Congressional source, it was learned that the President had mentioned the possibility of a joint session of Congress tomorrow. This naturally led to speculation that the Chief Executive would address it and ask in person, as did Woodrow Wilson in 1917, that it declare war.

Turn to Page B, Column 1

On Dec. 8, the Navy recruiting office in San Francisco was swamped with men hoping to enlist. LC-USF34-81861-E

bit more grim and sobering, for he also spoke of "American ships . . . torpedoed on the high seas between San Francisco and Honolulu." "Hostilities exist," Roosevelt continued. "There is no blinking at the fact that our people, our territory, and our interests are in grave danger." Certainly graver for at least one part of the nation—or so it seemed to the people of the West Coast, whose beaches were washed by the very "high seas between San Francisco and Honolulu" and whose cities faced perhaps the gravest danger from aerial bombardment.

Events later in the day appeared to confirm Roosevelt's concern for the Pacific Coast. At 7:00 P.M. the Western Defense Command restricted all radio stations from Seattle to San Diego to a single 60-second broadcast each 15 minutes and later to a one-minute transmission each half-hour. The next day, all stations were ordered off the air entirely to prevent enemy bombers from fixing on broadcast sources. Los Angeles' 90 aircraft warning and listening posts were placed on a 24-hour operating schedule. All the R.O.T.C. equipment at UCLA was moved to military centers.

In the midst of state and local activity, the federal government was also hard at work. By Dec. 8, U.S. Attorney General Francis Biddle had ordered more than 700 Japanese aliens detained by the FBI. In Southern California, the FBI detained 300 more in the Terminal Island immigration station for identification and questioning. Biddle discounted rumors of a wholesale roundup of Japanese aliens or Japanese Americans. "Less than 1,000 Japanese nationals will be affected," he told the press. "Procedures are being established to provide a fair hearing for all." Nevertheless, by Dec. 9, the number of detainees had swelled to 1,291; all were arrested without formal charges.

With the declaration of war by the other Axis powers, the FBI's list was expanded to include German and Italian nationals. In California the Bureau arrested 10 Italians and 70 Germans, among them Hermann Schwinn, the West Coast head of the German-American Bund. The FBI also confiscated a quantity of German literature, pictures and Schwinn's camera. Nationwide, 865 Germans and 147 Italians had been arrested by Dec. 9.

In Seattle, a crowd of more than 1,000 people enforced the city's first wartime blackout by smashing store windows when lights were not extinguished. The self-appointed wardens marched righteously through the center of the business district, shattering plate-glass shop windows and looting a six-block area. Nineteen-year-old Ethel Chelsvig, the wife of a seaman aboard a U.S. destroyer, told police, "If I could have found a brick, I, too, would had thrown it. We've got to show these people that they can't leave their lights burning. This is war. They don't realize that one light in the city might betray us. That's my patriotism."

But on Dec. 9, the mood in Seattle was even grimmer. The Pacific Northwest was about to become the front lines—or so believed Andrew McGavring, the mayor of Victoria, B.C., when he precipitously announced: "The Japanese are off the Aleutian Islands." Canadian Air Commodore A.E. Godfrey called the situation serious, adding, "There is every reason to believe there will be an attack on our area." Seattle residents were doubly alarmed: News of the alleged and impending attack came in the middle of a blackout as they huddled around their radios. "People who had pooh-poohed any hint of peril on Sunday," observed journalist Richard Neuberger, "kept their children home from school on Monday."

The Western Defense Command ordered blackouts for Tacoma and Walla Walla, Washington; a heavy fog lay over Spokane, making a real blackout unnecessary. Throughout Washington, radio stations were ordered

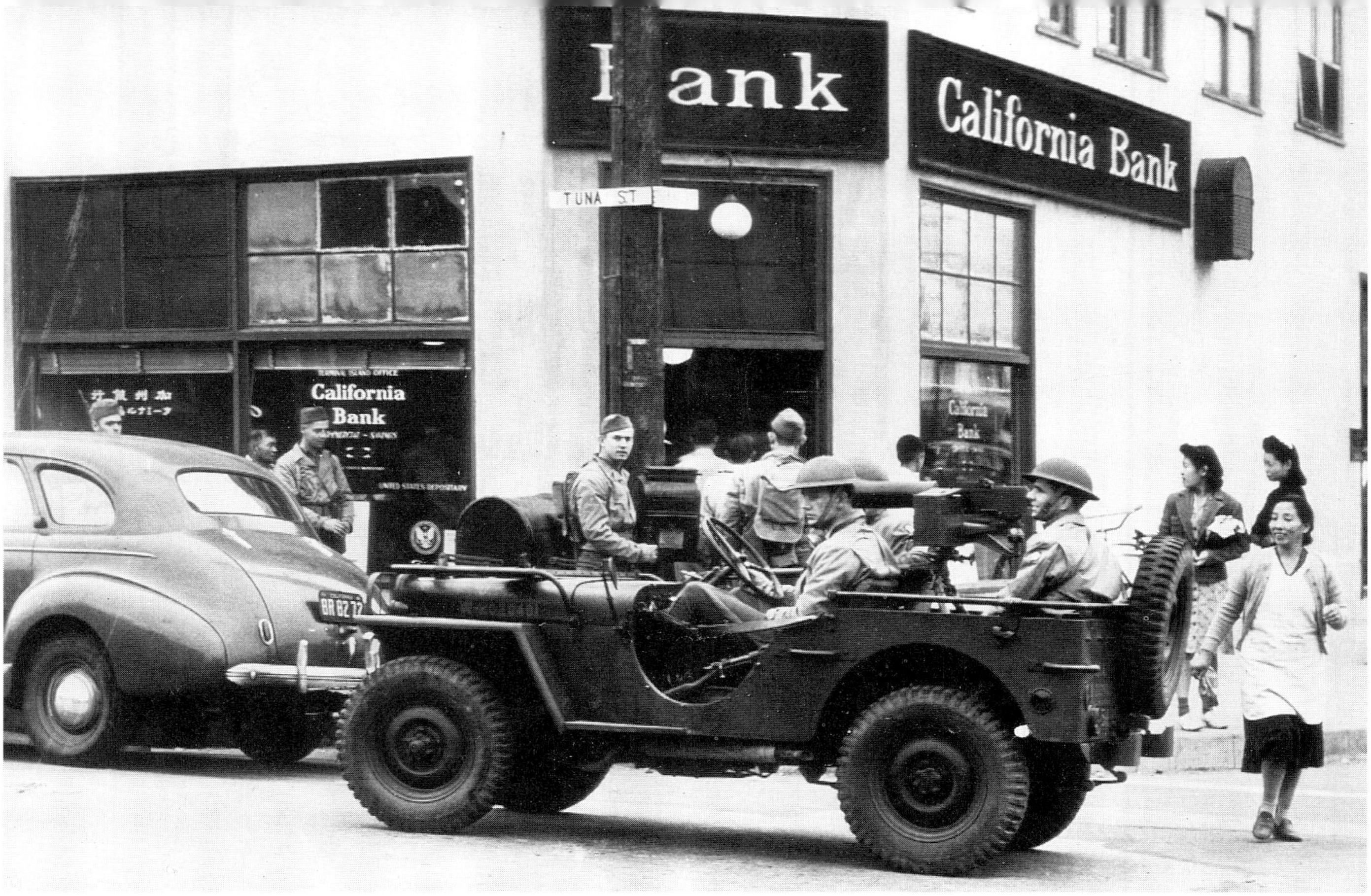
California Bank
TUNA ST
California
Bank

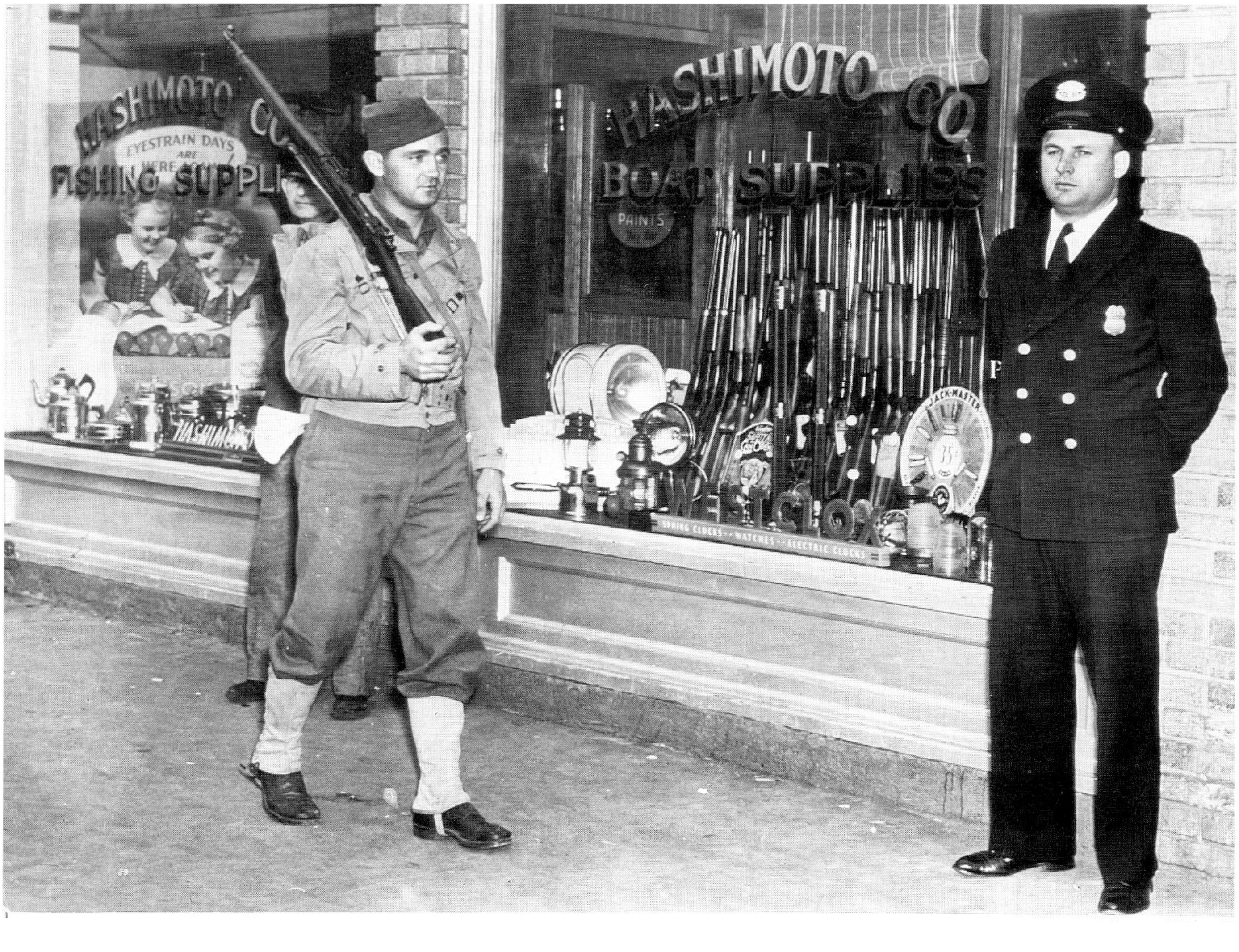
HASHIMOTO CO
BOAT SUPPLIES
PAINTS
WESTCLOX
SPRING CLOCKS • WATCHES • ELECTRIC CLOCKS

FACING PAGE: On Dec. 8 soldiers moved into the Japanese community on Terminal Island, San Pedro, California. Hundreds of anxious Japanese-Americans, seeking to ascertain the effect of new monetary regulations imposed by the government, flocked to banks in the area (*top photo*). A Japanese-American-owned sporting goods and hardware store was closed by the U.S. Customs Service. ABOVE: Sandbags were piled to the second story of the telephone company's building in San Francisco as protection in the event of an air raid, December 1941. AT RIGHT: Windows of the San Francisco Bank, one of the city's oldest banking institutions, get a black coating in conformity with air raid blackout regulations, Dec. 12, 1941.

off the air. Only KIRO, the 50,000-watt Seattle station remained open for official announcements. Guards were tripled at the Grand Coulee and Bonneville dams.

In the Bay Area, the counties of San Francisco, Alameda and Contra Costa went on an immediate 24-hour war footing, as individual defense councils met in hurried sessions late Sunday afternoon. In Emeryville, where the federal government had been rushing millions of dollars worth of orders through vital defense industries, plants were immediately blacked out, and armed sentries were posted. The huge Paraffine Company stationed guards every 200 feet. Other armed troops augmented the already heavy guard positioned around the Army Quartermaster Supply Depot. More than 300 veterans of World War I were detailed to 24-hour guard duty by Albany Chief of Police L.G. Lester. Four-hour watches were posted at such vital points as the Eastshore Highway overpass, Southern Pacific railway tracks, and the newly built, $2 million government-owned Western Research Laboratory. Guards were also stationed at various East Bay telephone exchanges.

Fire and police departments went on immediate 12-hour shifts, and all leaves were cancelled. The Posey Tube, linking Alameda and Oakland, would henceforth be closed to civilian traffic each night from 6:00 P.M. to 6:00 A.M. Patrolmen were stationed at all estuary bridges and at both entrances to the tube to halt and inspect all cars containing Japanese and to confiscate any weapons or cameras. The two famous bridges in the Bay Area, the San Francisco-Oakland Bay and the Golden Gate, were immediately posted with sentries checking everyone who crossed. Twelve miles west of the Golden Gate, the famous lightship *San Francisco*, a mariners' landmark for more than 30 years, was called into port immediately. She would not return to her station for nearly four years.

During the night of Dec. 8, 30 unidentified planes were reported approaching the Bay Area.[2] Mayor Angelo Rossi of San Francisco confirmed the information with the military authorities and ordered all radio stations off the air and a complete blackout of the city. But thousands of motorists drove to the Oakland Hills to view the blackout or perhaps see the first aerial combat over the Bay Area. Police had their hands full stopping motorists and warning them to turn out their headlights. Merchants were ordered to extinguish

Units of the California State Guard, carrying full equipment, set up guard posts and patrols on the Golden Gate Bridge to prevent possible sabotage to the important structure, Dec. 8, 1941.

---

[2]. "The official explanation was that 30 enemy planes had flown in from the south, passing over Mare Island Naval Base, then split into two groups over the city, one group flying north, the other south. Army pursuits tracked the northbound group for a time but lost it; the southern group was never located. Actually there had been no hostile planes." (Richard J. Lingeman, *Don't You Know There's a War On? The American Home Front, 1941-1945* [New York: G.P. Putnam's Sons, 1979], p. 26.). General DeWitt believed otherwise: "I don't think there's any doubt the planes came from a carrier," he said the day after the reported attack.

The California State Automobile Association put up 3,000 signs in Northern California.

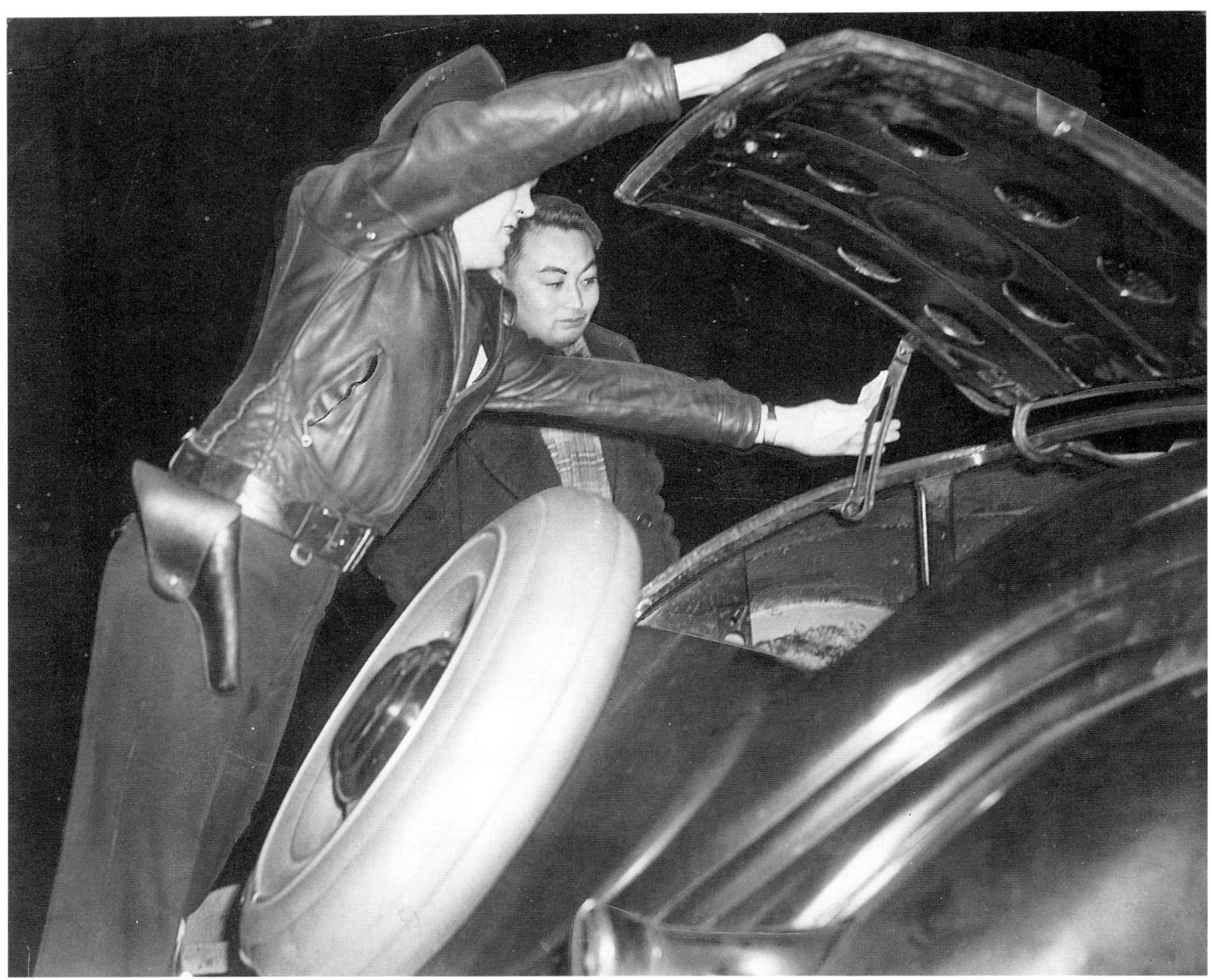

On Dec. 8, all cars carrying Japanese-Americans crossing the Bay Bridge were searched before being allowed to cross to San Francisco.

their lighted signs and Christmas decorations. Some city officials suggested the electric company pull its main switches, turning out every light in the area. But military authorities hastened to explain that all the telephones and police radios would also lose power.

Throughout the night, there were reports of antiaircraft gunfire, although later reports confirmed that no shots were fired. But searchlights played across the skies from the hills around the Bay Area and were visible as far south as San Jose and as far north as San Rafael. Confusion reigned throughout San Francisco. The Presidio remained in darkness, but Alcatraz Island was lighted like a huge birthday cake; officials were reluctant to darken the prison for fear it would aid an escape. Motorists crossing the Bay and Golden Gate bridges witnessed the sodium vapor lights suddenly flicker out. Highway patrolmen ordered all drivers to turn off their headlights and proceed slowly. Traffic on the darkened spans crawled very slowly that night.

The blackouts inspired a variety of individual ingenuity. Because no one could see in the total darkness, it was suggested that luminous strips of cloth be attached to clothing. Hollywood star Maria Montez posed for a photograph showing a bell hung under her shoe between the high heel and the toe. This, she claimed, would produce a tingling sound and identify her presence. None of the innovations ever were adopted.

The Bay Area's first blackout was a dubious success at best. The exercise included the Pacific Coast northward as far as the Canadian border, and it proceeded erratically, never producing complete darkness. San Francisco's efforts were compounded by traffic accidents, as cars and trucks, with only their parking lights for illumination, produced confusion and congestion and the deaths of three people. The next morning, angered and disgusted by the blackout fizzles up and down the coast, Lieutenant General John DeWitt, commanding general of the Fourth Army (which extended from Alaska to Mexico) and the Western Defense Command, lashed out at the complacent citizens of the Bay Area. The apoplectic DeWitt announced that unless the area observed proper air-raid precautions, civilian deaths would result. "If I can't knock

LEFT: Shelter signs appeared in all the major cities along the West Coast.
BELOW: Camera equipment of a Japanese-American family is inspected by a patrolman in Oakland, California. He was either taking film out of the cameras or confiscating them.

Anti-aircraft guns take up positions near the Golden Gate Bridge.

it into them with words," he warned at a conference of San Francisco's civilian defense leaders, "we'll have to turn it over to the police to knock it in with clubs. When the alarm sounds it means that an air raid is threatened. Those planes were over the Bay Area a definite length of time. They were enemy planes and I mean Japanese planes. They were detected and followed to sea. I hate to say this but it might have been a good thing if bombs had been dropped to wake you all up. San Francisco woke up this morning without a death from bombing. Suppose we had started to shoot? If an enemy had not dropped bombs and there had been a signal for aircraft fire, death would have been all around because our boys would have been firing at any kind of light, even horizontal. So put out your lights and take it. If you can't take it, get out of San Francisco."

Instructions to all citizens, about proper air-raid conduct were quickly printed in the newspapers and broadcast on the radio, carefully identifying the alarm signals and explaining what to do when they sounded. Bay Area citizens received the following instructions:

"The modulated wail of a siren for a two-minute period will be the signal for the blackout and to take cover. The signal will be given approximately seven minutes before the planes are expected overhead, but there may be occasions when much less warning time will be given. 'All Clear' will be sounded by the blowing of the same sirens or whistles at the same pitch for two minutes. This is what you are instructed to do. Stay at home. Turn out the house lights. When bombs fall, lie down on the floor away from the path of flying glass or other fragments. Normally the basement is a safe place to be. Motorists should pull into the curb, turn out lights, get under cover and lie down. Stay off the streets and out of crowded places. If incendiary bombs fall on your home, cover them with dry sand. Keep sand bags in your home. Keep a garden hose attached to the faucet if possible. Play only a fine spray of water on bombs. A jet or splash will explode them.

"Fill your bath tubs and all buckets with water under raid conditions in the event water mains are broken. Locate the nearest fire alarm box and use it instead of a telephone. If there is a gas attack, go to the room in your house with the least number of doors and windows. Paste paper over the windows, stuff cracks in the doors and windows with rags. Keep blacked out until the all clear signal."

On Wednesday, Dec. 10, Eleanor Roosevelt, the assistant director of the Office of Civilian Defense, arrived in San Francisco with Mayor Rossi, General DeWitt, and other area authorities. The next morning she would leave for similar conferences in Portland, Tacoma and Seattle.

Federal Bureau of Investigation agents were studying motion pictures taken by a San Francisco woman which purported to show signal lights flashed to enemy ships during Monday night's blackout. There was still no explanation of the flares reportedly dropped during the same air-raid alarm. The Army Air Command refused to comment except to say they did not come from American airplanes.

Early the next morning, Northern California had its first evacuations. More than 300 patients from the Fort Riley Veterans' Hospital at the Presidio and all Army dependents from McClellan Air Base outside Sacramento were also moved to safer locations.

During the next few days, preparedness for a Japanese invasion reached a peak. In Marin County the toughest ordinance yet devised was passed. Any person showing a light during an air-raid alert would face a $500 fine and a six-month jail sentence. Lights visible for more than 100 feet and that could not be turned out in less than one minute would have to be turned off for the duration of the war. Department stores and other businesses announced they would close early every day to allow employees to get home before blackout time. Civilian defense officials designated certain buildings as public air-raid shelters, and signs indicating their locations quickly appeared in the

A practice alert to repulse an enemy attack. They are still wearing World War One helmets.

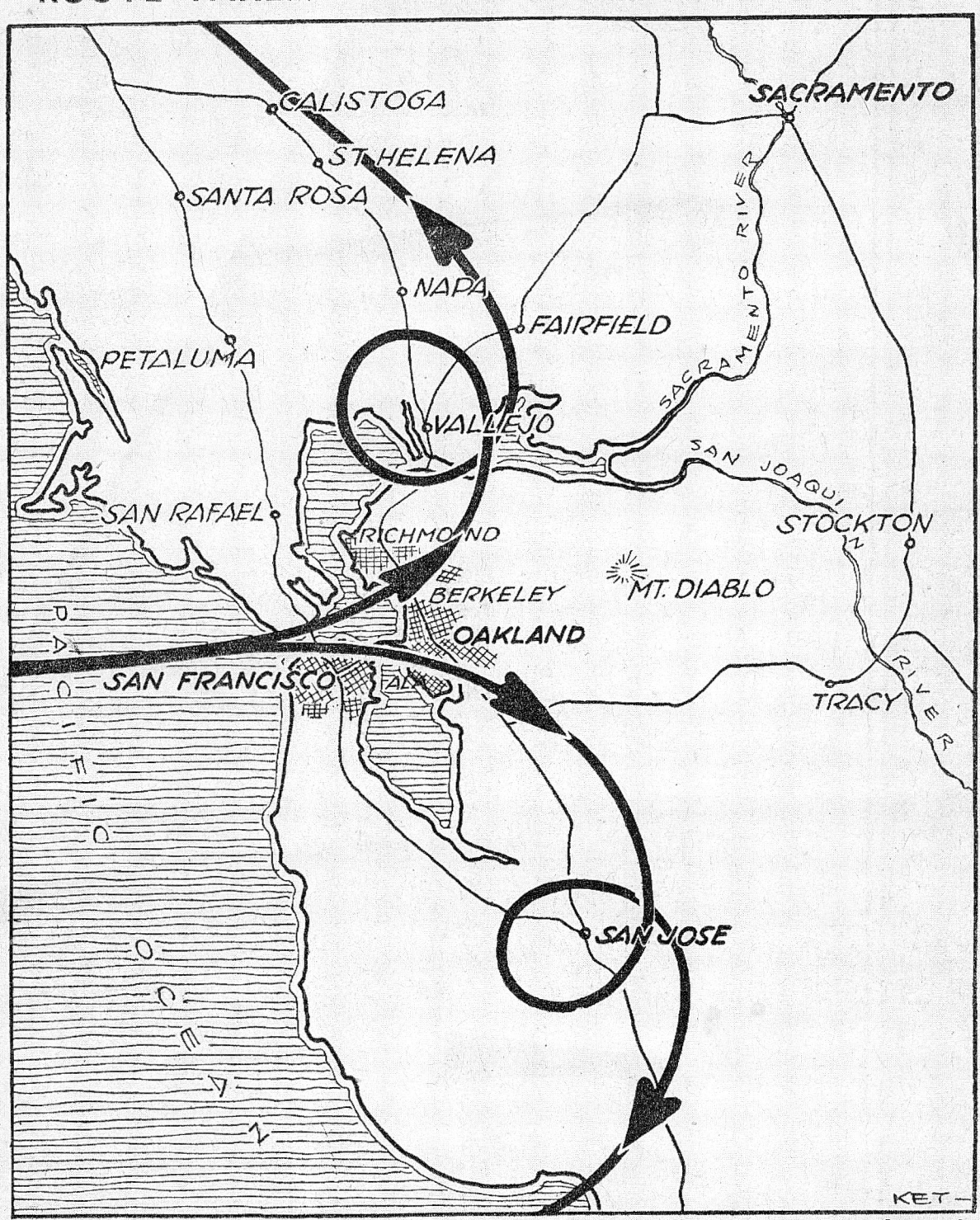

The dotted lines on this map of the Bay Area show the course followed by two squadrons of Japanese bombers reported by the Army over this area last night. They split and one group circled San Jose before disappearing to the southwest. The other squadron passed over Mare Island and then headed north toward Mendocino County. No planes were caught.

This appeared in a San Francisco newspaper. It of course never occurred.

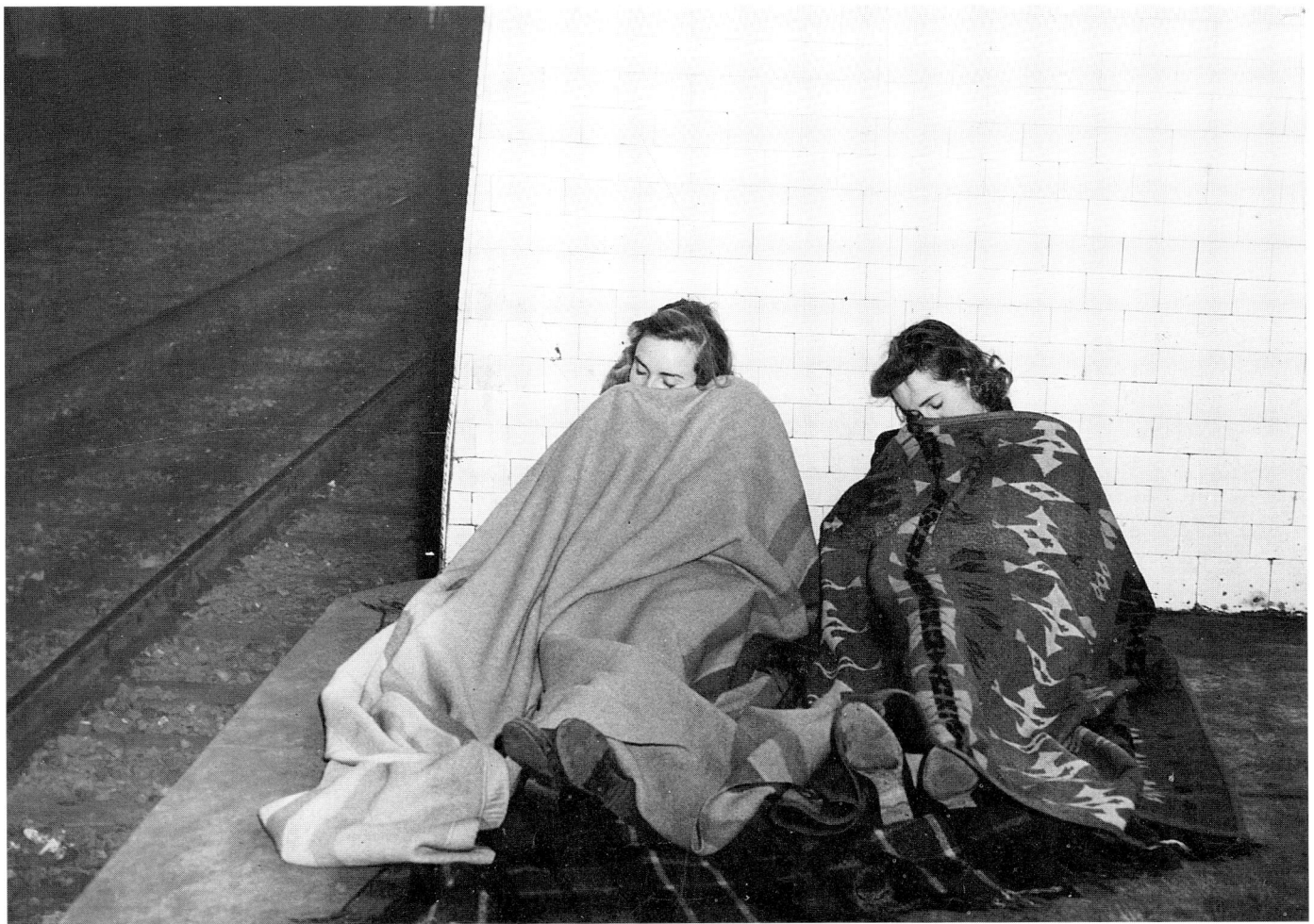

Although the second night of partial blackout conditions in San Francisco had air raid signals and streetlights on, some residents played it safe by using some of the trolley tunnel stations as shelters, like this one under Twin Peaks. A few hours on concrete floors and benches caused these people to go back to their homes, Dec. 9, 1941.

downtown areas of every West Coast city. Many people began constructing their own air-raid shelters in basements and back yards.

Anyone leaving the coastal metropolitan areas and heading East over the mountain roads found them closed or their car searched by the highway patrol. Commercial fishing fleets were quickly placed under the protection of the U.S. Coast Guard, whose cutters shepherded the fleet in and out of port. Japanese-American fishermen were forbidden to practice their trade.

In Southern California, the Army Air Corps assumed control of the blackouts from the navy, immediately halting the practice alerts in Los Angeles and Long Beach harbors. The alerts were disrupting the 24-hour operation of the shipyards. Factory and business operators from Santa Barbara to San Ysidro painted over their windows.

Invasion fever hit the Southland two days after Pearl Harbor. By the evening of Dec. 9, Los Angeles had been allegedly and variously threatened by:
· 11 unidentified warplanes approaching from the sea;
· 34 Japanese naval vessels lurking off Manhattan Beach, waiting for a fog to lift before attacking;
· a "Japanese cruiser 20,000 yards off the western tip of Catalina Island;" and
· three Japanese destroyers and one cruiser somewhere off the Palos Verdes Peninsula.

Three of the reports were confirmed false alarms; the 34 vessels menacing Manhattan Beach were Terminal Island fishermen.

The first full-blown air-raid alarm in Southern California occurred on the evening of Dec. 10 and extended from Bakersfield to Tijuana to Boulder Dam. The Army's Fourth Interceptor Command ordered a blackout at 7:45 p.m., alarmed because unidentified planes were reportedly approaching Los Angeles from the ocean—perhaps the same phantom aircraft that had menaced the Bay Area the night before. All radio stations were ordered off the air, and by 8:00 the blackout was pronounced near perfect in all nearby localities—except in Los Angeles itself where conditions were termed "spotty." Searchlights near the Los Angeles harbor and at the aircraft plants in Inglewood crisscrossed the skies, searching in vain for Japanese warplanes; none were found. But for Angelinos the war was nonetheless a much closer and frightening reality.

The war came quickly to the U.S. Weather Bureau. Employees were ordered to discontinue issuing all weather forecasts. Weather predictions were considered military information. The only exception was the weekly report on the condition of snow in recreational areas.

Fiorello H. LaGuardia came to the West Coast and declared he was "not satisfied with the civilian defense operations anywhere," although he did add that the West Coast was far ahead of Great Britain at a corresponding period of the European war. "We're at war with a strong enemy," said LaGuardia, "and we've got work to do, a lot of work, and no time to waste. It's going to be a very difficult war. It's going to be a long war. We are going to win, but we've got to fight with all we have."

When casualty figures from Pearl Harbor were released, the nation was shocked. There was a total of 2,251 killed and 1,119 wounded, along with 68 civilians killed by falling anti-aircraft shells. Eighty-six ships of the U.S. Navy were anchored in Pearl Harbor that morning. Fortunately, a two-carrier task force was at sea, not involved in the attack. The Japanese task force consisted of 441 planes and five midget submarines. Their major targets were the large battleships at anchor with minimal guards on duty. The *Arizona* was destroyed. Four other battleships, three destroyers, one target ship, and a mine layer were seriously damaged. Three additional battleships and three cruisers were also damaged but eventually repaired. The Navy lost 92 planes and the Army 96—in all, a tremendous setback to our military potential. The Japanese lost only 29.

Organized only a few months before the Pearl Harbor attack, California State Guard were called into action on Dec. 8. They were posted as guards on the San Francisco waterfront. Here guardsmen have stopped a car entering Pier 14 occupied by the American Railway Express Company.

Ellis O. Jones and Robert Noble (right), leaders of two isolationist organizations, were arrested on April 1, 1942, in Los Angeles by FBI agents on sedition charges. Agents searched Noble's home based on state charges that he criminally libeled Gen. Douglas MacArthur.

Other news was equally grim. The Japanese had landed in the Philippines, Guam, Hong Kong and Malaya. This meant Great Britain, already under the strain of war in Europe, was now involved in Southeast Asia with the Japanese. Reports from the Philippines told of bombing raids on Manila and the Cavite Naval Base. Stories of fifth-columnist fishermen aiding the Japanese army to land on Lubang Island near the entrance to Manila Bay raised fears of similar activities on the West Coast. The Japanese also bombed Midway and Wake islands.

On Dec. 10, the British Admiralty announced the loss of two of her mightiest ships, the 35,000-ton battleship *Prince of Wales* and the 32,000-ton cruiser *Repulse*, both sunk off the coast of Malaya. Further details of the battle were not forthcoming, but a Japanese communiqué claimed the ships were sunk by aircraft—a claim eventually proved true. The loss of *Prince of Wales* and *Repulse* sent shock waves through the Allied military commands. These ships were the strongest of the British fleet, and naval vessels of their size had never before been sunk in wartime by aircraft bombardment. American bravado prompted by Pearl Harbor began to sound a bit hollow; our enemy in the Pacific was formidable indeed—and far more so than we expected.

But war fever and patriotism had captured the nation nonetheless—but not *all* of the nation. Some Americans were quite outspoken in their bitterness toward their country and attracted a good deal of attention from the Justice Department. On Thursday, Dec. 11, about 200 people attended a public meeting in the Embassy Auditorium in Los Angeles. Ellis O. Jones, the leader of the Copperheads, a group formed originally to criticize Lincoln's conduct of the Civil War, declared the Japanese had a right to Hawaii. There were, after all, more Japanese there than Americans. "I would rather be in the war on the side of Germany than on the side of the British," Jones declared. Another speaker, Robert Noble, said, "Our country has not been attacked. Japan has done a good job in the Pacific. I believe the war is going to destroy America." At the close of the meeting, the audience voted to impeach President Roosevelt, depicted by a wax-faced dummy. Later that night, agents of the U.S. District Attorney's office arrested Jones and Noble and charged them with sedition. Bail was set at $25,000 but was reduced to $500; the two were finally released on Dec. 22 on orders of the Justice Department.

But Jones and Noble immediately resumed anti-American and pro-Axis agitation. Their organization, Friends of Progress, held weekly meetings in downtown Los Angeles where they distributed handbills stating, "Young men, your lowest aim in life is to be a good soldier" and "How you can legally keep out of the war effort." From the platform Noble continued his admiration of the enemy. On Feb. 23 he told a legislative committee, "The Japanese did the proper thing under the exigencies of the time when they bombed Pearl Harbor. Now it is all over in the Pacific and we might as well come home." The following month, California Attorney General Earl Warren had them arrested again for asserting in a Copperhead newsletter that General MacArthur's departure from the Philippines was desertion. The two were charged with criminal libel but later, again, released.

Other groups with similar convictions—including the World Events Forum, the National Legion of Mothers and Women of America, and certain units of the former America First Committee—also operated in Los Angeles. Pro-Axis readers could also subscribe to two blatantly anti-Semitic publications, San Diego's *Broom* and William Kullgren's *Beam Light*, published in Atascadero near Camp Roberts. Using astrological signs, editor Kullgren predicted a wave of pogroms for American Jews and Roosevelt's death at the hands of an assassin.

San Francisco, the famous old lightship from the early 1900s, was called into port immediately after the Pearl Harbor attack. In October 1945, the ship resumed her position 12 miles due west of the "Golden Gate."

California's pro-Axis groups were closely monitored by the Justice Department—and the American Legion—and, though vocal, never became a serious threat to the nation. On the West Coast, their polemics were scarcely noticed as war preparations and jitters continued to dominate everyday life throughout December.

All night trains on the Pacific Coast were running with drawn window shades and greatly reduced headlights. Mexico, though theoretically not at war with Japan, cooperated with the American authorities by blacking out its border cities on the coast. Mexican Army officers pointed out that San Diego's blackout would be ineffective if Tijuana's lights were visible 20 miles away.

The likelihood grew that the West Coast would adopt Daylight Saving Time, thereby dropping its long opposition to what had become standard practice in the East. This would allow more people to return home from work while the skies were still light. Wholesale houses and stores sold out of black cotton cloth, used for darkening windows during blackouts. Blue lightbulbs sold out quickly and merchants also moved huge quantities of black paint, not only to darken windows but also to cover metal roofs that reflected moonlight.

The roundup of aliens continued throughout California and the West. By Friday, Dec. 12, 178 additional Axis nationals in the Bay Area had been taken into custody by the FBI; this total included 101 Japanese, 59 Germans and 18 Italians. Although the FBI maintained silence regarding the identity of the persons arrested, they were all alleged to be leaders within their respective communities. In Berkeley, U.S. Treasury Department agents froze the assets of nine cleaning establishments owned by Japanese. A spokesman for the Japanese American Citizens League in San Francisco advised members to avoid public places of amusement and not congregate on the streets.

On the evening of the same day, a misinterpretation of Army orders led to the evacuation of 7,000 to 10,000 people living along a 40-mile stretch of the beaches near Santa Cruz. An Army lieutenant instructed all residents within 1,000 yards of the waterline to evacuate; in actuality the order read "All fishermen, squatters, and stragglers." People took shelter in theaters, schools and homes of friends. Because of the blackout, no automobile traffic was allowed, thereby forcing the evacuees to flee on foot. Fortunately, the evacuation ended a few hours later. But the inconvenience gave Santa Cruz the dubious distinction of being the first West Coast community to conduct a mass evacuation.

After attacking Pearl Harbor, the Japanese Sixth Fleet ordered nine of its large *I*-class submarines to attack shipping along the West Coast. Eight were equipped to carry small planes, although there is no evidence that they launched any during their December operations. Arriving off the West Coast, the submarines dispersed to nine patrol stations from Seattle to San Diego. There they remained for about a week, attacking coastal shipping.

The first submarine attack on West Coast shipping occurred on Saturday, Dec. 20. On that day, the Richfield Oil Company tanker *Agwiworld* put into Santa Cruz, 80 miles south of the Golden Gate, reporting that a large Japanese submarine (the *I-23*) had surfaced 20 miles off Cypress Point and fired eight rounds from her deck guns, hitting the tanker once in the side. The General Petroleum Company tanker *Emidio* was not as fortunate. On that same day, six rounds from the deck guns of the Japanese submarine *I-17* forced the crew of the San Pedro-bound vessel to

LEFT: First Lady Mrs. Eleanor Roosevelt was the assistant director of the Office of Civilian Defense under former New York City mayor, Fiorello H. La Giardia. She visited the west coast a few days after the Pearl Harbor attack to assess the civil defense preparations. Here she is shown with Brig. Gen. Frank W. Weed, Commanding General of Letterman General Hospital at the Presidio of San Francisco on Oct. 2, 1942. RIGHT: Offices in San Francisco that had to be open at night are prepared for wartime blackout conditions.

In the event of an air raid, citizens were advised to seek the best shelter possible. Here a mother and two children sit under a sturdy table with a chair propped up in front.

abandon ship within sight of Blunt's Reef off Cape Mendocino, 200 miles north of San Francisco. *Emidio* did not sink, but her survivors watched helplessly as the crippled tanker drifted onto the rocks near Crescent City. Farther south, another oil tanker, the *Larry Doheney*, was shelled by a Japanese submarine 20 miles off the coast of San Luis Obispo.[3]

After each attack, squadrons of Army and Navy scout planes took to the air in search of the submarines. News of the incidents came shortly after Rear Admiral John W. Greenslade, commandant of the 12th Naval District, said enemy submarines were actively searching for American ships off the Pacific Coast. These three attacks were the first reported in the Pacific since the sinking of the lumber freighter *Cynthia Olson*, torpedoed by a Japanese submarine 1,000 miles out of San Francisco on Dec. 7. In addition to attacking *Emidio*, *Larry Doheney* and *Agwiworld*, enemy submarines also fired on the lumber carrier *Samoa* off Santa Barbara, but she managed to twist out of the way of the torpedo.

Thus it would come as no surprise to the West Coast when Navy Secretary Frank Knox affirmed the next day that a fleet of 40 long-range Japanese submarines was operating off the Pacific Coast.[4] "Each submarine," Knox said, "could range 14,000 to 16,000 miles from their home base in the Marshall Islands and could cruise the West Coast for weeks at a time." To boost West Coast morale Knox also announced that American naval vessels were dealing effectively with the threat.

---

3. *Larry Doheney*'s luck lasted only until the next fall. On Oct. 5, 1942, the Japanese submarine *I-25* sent her to the bottom, five miles off Cape Sebastian, Oregon. *Emidio* lay on the rocks until well after the war. She was finally cut up for scrap in 1957.

4. Knox' figures were exaggerated; only nine Japanese submarines patrolled the West Coast.

During a two-hour, 40-minute blackout in San Francisco, these pictures were taken with infrared film and new blackout globes. These people are looking skyward for enemy planes on Dec. 13, 1941.

Surrounded by enthusiastic members of the Junior Victory Army, Sam Murray signs up bicycle corps at his shop in San Francisco. Couriers needed by the Office of Civilian Defense were supplied through the Junior Army.

Civilian patrolmen were given a two-week training course in the defense against chemical attack.

Top: School children of the 74th Street School in Los Angeles take bedding bags to school where they would be needed if they had to remain in the building during an air raid, Dec. 18, 1941. Bottom: A practice air raid drill at James Denman Junior High School, San Francisco. The students were required to sit on the floor of a corridor on the lowest level of the school with a clear lane between them until the "All Clear" sounded.

But not effectively enough to help the lumber freighter *Absaroka*, torpedoed by the Japanese submarine *I-19* on Christmas Eve off San Pedro. Observers on the shore watched as the submarine surfaced briefly, then disappeared. *Absaroka*, her decks at the waterline and listing badly, limped into port. A few days later, actress Jane Russell posed for photographers inside the gaping torpedo hole, holding a sign warning that "A slip of the lip may sink a ship." The words "may sink" were crossed out and the words "has sunk" substituted.

That same Christmas Eve, West Coast newspapers carried the story of the U.S. Marines' surrender of Wake Island to the Japanese. On Christmas Day the Japanese overwhelmed Hong Kong and were about to capture Manila in the Philippines. Nearby, on the Bataan Peninsula, U.S. and Philippine forces joined in an historic battle that would last until May 6, when the island fortress of Corregidor finally fell to the Japanese.

On Dec. 31, the U.S. Coast Guard ship *Hermes* off Point Montara picked up the sound of a submarine. *Hermes* dropped depth charges, and after about 45 minutes, the sound was no longer detectable. The surface was covered with a reddish brown oil slick indicating the submarine may have been hit.

The next day at 4:00 A.M., the 440-foot Union Oil tanker *Montebello* was sunk off the central California coast in heavy fighting. None of the crew was lost, although the submarine deck crew machine-gunned the lifeboats and shelled a fishing boat attempting to rescue the survivors. Residents of nearby coastal towns were awakened by the sounds of gunfire. The crew—wet, cold and numb—barely made it to shore. The military determined this was the same submarine that had attacked the *Doheny* earlier. Rumors spread that American bombers had finished off these Japanese submarines. However, these rumors were due more to wishful thinking than any solid evidence.

The Navy had little to say about the attacks, except to say the Japanese appeared to be very poor shots. Naval spokesmen pointed out that the submarines had thus far sunk only two unarmed merchant vessels. Unofficially, the Navy speculated the Japanese had

In preparation for the day when poison gas may fall on San Francisco, 16,900 gas masks were sent from Washington, D.C., to equip the city's protective services and Civilian Defense workers.

"buck fever." Far from their home bases, they feared planes and surface ships and did not take enough time for a careful attack. Captains of the ships facing attacks said they could have sunk the submarines had they been armed. Most of the time the Japanese submarines surfaced and used their deck guns to conserve torpedoes.

The attack on Pearl Harbor produced yet another threat to the West Coast. A two-man Japanese submarine was beached on Oahu during the Sunday morning attack. It was described as a suicide vessel that could be driven torpedo-like at an objective. The tiny submarine carried two 18-inch torpedoes and a 300-pound explosive charge. But their short cruising range (200 miles) required a mother ship for fuel and ammuni-

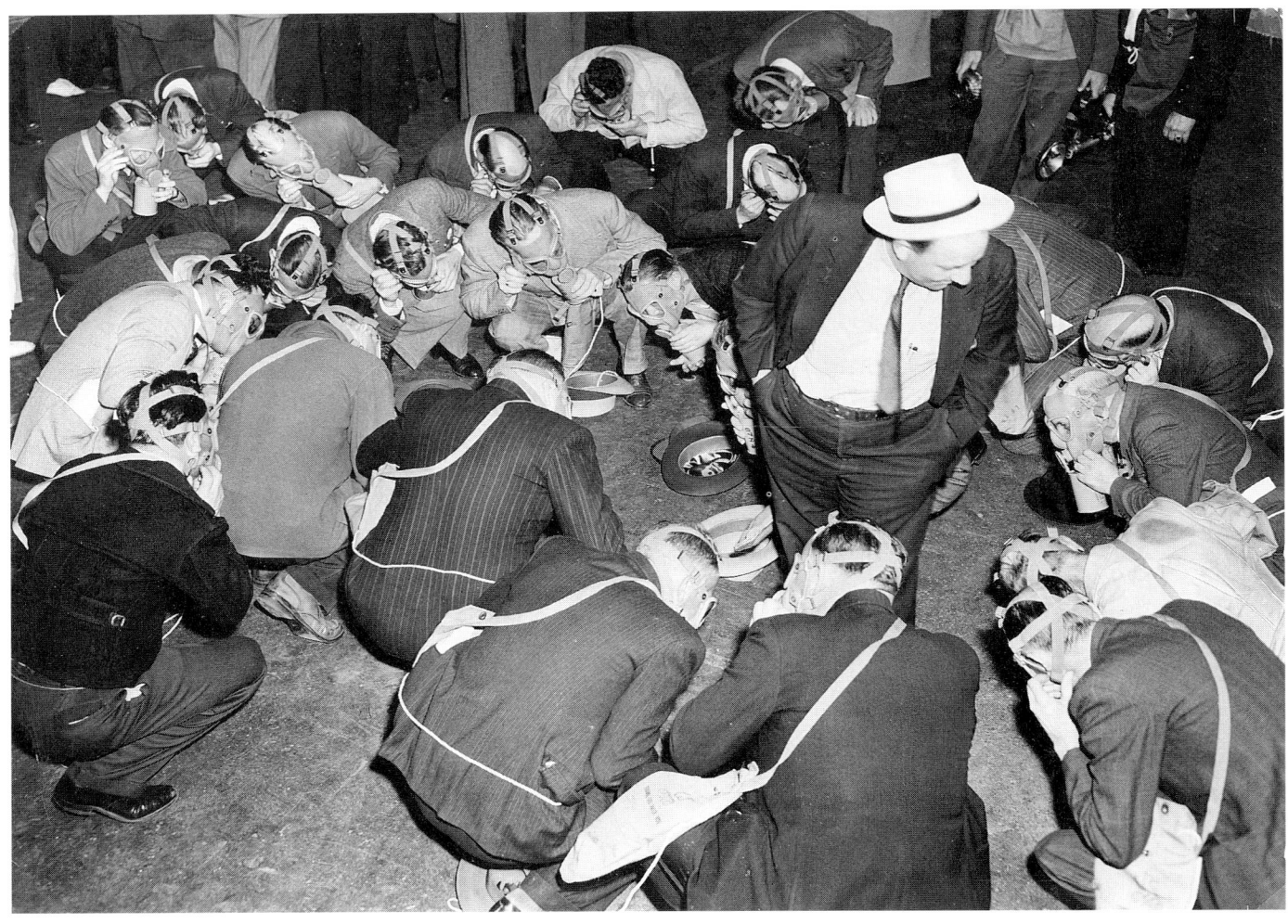
Instructions were given to air raid wardens in the use of gas masks. This group is rehearsing taking them off. They are crouched close to the floor to avoid stray gas.

tion. This threat and the presence of the larger *I*-class submarines prompted the Navy to construct an anti-submarine net in San Francisco Bay. Held down with 25-ton concrete anchors, this handmade cable screen stretched three and one-half miles across the bay, just inside the Golden Gate.

Throughout the end of December and into January, troops, guns, planes and equipment poured into the three western coastal states. Up and down the coast, the fear of invasion was palpable. "Like characters in a tremendous and terrible mystery story," *Life* magazine said, "the people of the United States Pacific Coast waited for something to happen. They didn't know what. They feared almost anything. Maybe the Japanese would bomb San Francisco, Portland or Seattle. Maybe Japanese planes would hedge-hop up from hidden bases on the peninsula of lower California and attack airplane factories of San Diego and Los Angeles. Maybe there would even be an enemy landing somewhere on the 1,300-mile coastline from Puget Sound to Mexico."[5]

Some senators urged the Army and Navy to pull in their forces and concentrate on defending the West Coast from invasion. But Secretary of War Stimson promised the United States would not disperse its forces defensively into small holding units. "West Coast residents," Stimson said, "were temperamentally suited to the offensive not the defensive. But we have to be prepared for attacks, not only far out in the Pacific, but along the California, Oregon and Washington coasts." In short, the West Coast must risk the possibility of a Japanese attack on its shores in order to later take the offensive and thus prevent a real invasion.

Nevertheless, in January the Office of Facts and Figures in Washington, D.C., was mapping out three scenarios of how the Japanese could invade the West Coast

5. "Pacific Coast Defense," *Life*, Jan. 12, 1942.

Employees of the Fireman's Fund Group in San Francisco practice putting out incendiary fires on the roof of their building. Firemen and their equipment were assigned to each of the buildings at 401 and 433 California and 233 Sansome streets. Equipment to fight incendiary bombs included shovels, shields, rakes, hoes, water sprays and sand.

On the roof of a San Francisco hotel, employees arrange sacks of sand to be opened and poured on incendiary bombs.

THE WEST COAST GOES TO WAR

An anti-submarine net was stretched across San Francisco Bay in 1941. In this 1945 photo, a net-tending vessel raises one of the 25-ton concrete anchors, which secured the handmade cable screen. The net was three and one-half miles long.

during the Spring of 1942. While the Office pointed out that it had no authoritative inside information either from Washington or elsewhere as to how or when the Japanese might strike, it said its conclusions were based on military logic and the enemy's past performance.

One plan called for the Japanese to skip across the northern Pacific, culminating in a surprise attack on the U.S. base at Dutch Harbor in the Aleutian Islands. This would entail Japanese aircraft carriers linking up with German battleships such as *Tirpitz* and *Schornhorst*. Presumably, this would give the Axis powers overwhelming naval superiority. The Japanese would then advance to Kodiak, Alaska, capturing air bases along the way. Their land-based planes would aid carrier planes in protecting the sea advance down along British Columbia and the West Coast of the U.S. This, the office predicted, would be coordinated with diversionary attacks on the East Coast.

Plan two called for an extremely difficult frontal attack on the West Coast via Pearl Harbor. Japanese troops, supported by carriers, would first land on the outer Hawaiian Islands, then set up air bases and close in on Oahu. The main drive would be directed at San Francisco, while feints would be made on Los Angeles, Seattle and the Panama Canal.

Plan three called for a southern Pacific crossing by the Japanese. Again the enemy fleet, reinforced by the Germans, would surprise bomb the Panama Canal, followed by a landing in Ecuador for an attack up the West Coast.

At the root of each hypothetical invasion plan were complex problems of logistics. But one fact seemed certain; the Japanese would try to conquer the West Coast while the U.S. was still assembling its great war machine. The month given by the Office of Facts and Figures for this invasion was April, a little more than 60 days away. The office issued the following scenario: A Japanese scout bomber would be spotted over the Aleutian Islands in mid-March. Within two weeks Alaska would fall to invading troops. By June, the Japanese would reach the great airplane factories in the Pacific Northwest. As one man, a hundred thousand Japanese, German and Italian fifth-columnists would rock Seattle, San Francisco and Los Angeles with explosives and other acts of sabotage.

There were rumors of Japanese fifth-column activities in Hawaii and the Philippines aiding Japanese forces in bombings and landings, though no such activity was subsequently proven. However, it lent credence to fears that similar acts would happen on the West Coast.

A ground crew raises one of the barrage balloons that have been placed on guard duty against possible enemy air raids along the Pacific Coast, June 1942.

The *SS Emidio,* the first ship torpedoed off the Pacific Coast by a Japanese submarine. It was hit on Dec. 19, 1941, off Eureka, Calif., and it floated to a beach near Crescent City, Calif., on Dec. 20.

Portions of the hull of the *SS Emidio* on display at Beachfront Park in Crescent City, Calif.

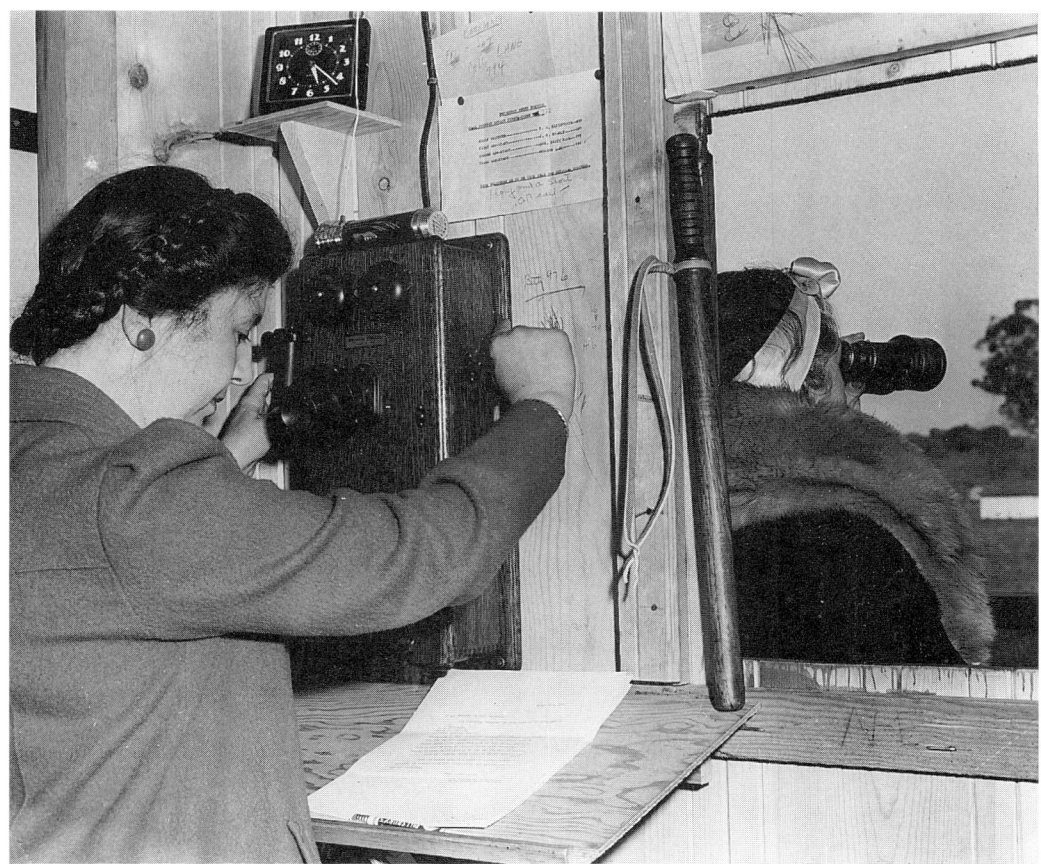

Some of the more remote observation posts on the West Coast still used the old-fashioned telephones, complete with side-winding bell. Note the policeman's billy club by the window.

Air raid warden areas in San Francisco were charted on a large map in the basement of City Hall.

Part of the battery of 40 telephones in the San Francisco Civil Defense center. Air Raid wardens would flash word of crisis in any part of the city in the event of air raids. The messages received would be relayed by the operators to Civil Defense agency executives in the same room, who in turn would communicate instructions by direct wire to their agencies, January 1942.

On the North Peak of Twin Peaks in San Francisco, workers mount a giant siren that would serve as an air raid warning system for the city, Dec. 18, 1941.

Somewhere in Los Angeles the army set up this Filter Board of the Aircraft Warning Service, through which information concerning all aircraft movements in the vicinity were directed to military authorities. Aircraft spotters in the area kept the board workers informed on courses of planes flying over territory indicated on the big map, Dec. 22, 1941.

Members of the Twin Peaks Post American Legion in San Francisco served as members of the U.S. Army Air Forces Aircraft Warning Service. The brassard was awarded after 100 hours of service; medals after 500.

From these two rooms all activities in Oakland could be controlled in case of an air raid.

AT RIGHT: Volunteer women and military personnel worked day and night around the operations board to protect the San Francisco area from enemy attack. Every flight of planes entering their zone of vigilance was checked and plotted on the master map.

BELOW: Young girls at work in the Seattle Aircraft Warning Service Center, Janaury 1942.

"Somewhere in the Pacific Northwest" a soldier stands guard in a beachhead machine gun emplacement, Feb. 4, 1942.

AT RIGHT: A 75 mm. gun crew guards a beach position somewhere along the West Coast, Feb. 12, 1942.

BELOW: Soldiers manning an aircraft detection instrument at an anti-aircraft battery in Northern California. The heater in the auxiliary dugout to the right adds a little comfort for the soldiers maintaining a continuous night and day alert, January 1942.

Another 75 mm. gun on guard against a possible enemy invasion, Dec. 23, 1941.

Typical of the seaward alert for enemy planes, this soldier kneels just outside his shelter foxhole, Dec. 19, 1941.

Members of the 32nd Infantry from Fort Ord have driven a jeep into a sloping hole to camouflage it. An air-cooled machine gun is mounted on top. This photo was taken in May 1941.

The first line of defense in the early months of the war.

One hundred thirty-six young naval recruits were on hand to form this big "V" in front of the federal building in Los Angeles. They were sworn in by Lt. Cmdr. James J. Tunney, former heavyweight boxing champion, who was making a national tour of recruiting stations, Oct. 31, 1941.

The first mobile canteen unit, which fed 2,500 people per hour on emergency meals of soup, stew and coffee, was demonstrated by the San Francisco chapter of the American Red Cross. The portable unit, intended for civilian relief in any disaster, was used to feed a group of soldiers in its first appearance in San Francisco, Jan. 18, 1942.

A P-40 fighter plane at Hamilton Field. Tin cans were tied on the barbed wire fence to give warning if saboteurs tried to cut the wire, March 1942.

An army convoy rolls through an Oakland street in August 1942.

Hollywood stars sit in a shelter on the Warner Brothers movie lot during a practice air raid drill on Jan. 4, 1942. Left to right: director Michael Curtiz, actor Dennis Morgan, actress Bette Davis, a studio workman, actress Irene Manning and another workman.

A soldier guards a sandbagged oil well pump in a southern California oil field. After the attack on Pearl Harbor, major industrial complexes along America's coastline were guarded by Army troops.

CHAPTER FOUR

Rainbow 5

MONTHS BEFORE the Japanese attack on Pearl Harbor, American military strategists had divided the continental United States into geographical defense commands. Contingency plans, to be enacted in the event of an enemy attack, were then devised for each area. The West Coast, under the command of General DeWitt at the Presidio, was part of the Western Defense Command, comprised of the eight Western states. Shortly after Japanese bombs began falling on Pearl Harbor, General Headquarters in Washington ordered DeWitt to implement "Rainbow 5," the contingency plan for the West Coast. In the Presidio communications room, teletype operators dispatched the Rainbow 5 order to military installations from Fort Rosecrans in San Diego to Fort Casey on Puget Sound. The West Coast began to mobilize.

By the afternoon of Dec. 7, while civilians remained close to their radios or anxiously scanned extra newspaper headlines, troops in every Army installation were called out and dispersed to Rainbow 5 defense positions. By 8:00 p.m., as West Coast radios tuned in the 'Jack Benny Show,' the coasts of Washington, Oregon and California were armed camps.

Within a week of Pearl Harbor, soldiers on 24-hour alert were bivouacked everywhere—in barns, dugouts, and hastily dug trenches. At every vantage point authorities set up observation and listening posts, as well as gun positions and fire-control stations. Tactical commands commandeered schools and vacation hotels for their headquarters. Along the coast, defense preparations were particularly intense: Nearly every yard of shoreline was within range of fixed machine guns or huge coastal cannons. Artillery and antiaircraft guns were carefully hidden from air observation. Even the famous Southern California beaches, where winter tourists romped in peace the week before, were masses of barbed wire, patrolled by serious troops. Los Angeles and Orange County beaches from Zuma to Dana Point were restricted after 5:00 p.m.—and would remain so for the war's duration.

Air raid defense rested on the cooperation between soldiers and civilians. The Army would man sound and radio locators and antiaircraft searchlights and guns. Civilians were responsible for insuring that blackouts were complete, to act as air raid wardens and messengers, man fire engines and ambulances, and otherwise remain calm and orderly. By Jan. 20, California had 136,400 civilian defense volunteers. Oregon had 39,000 and Washington had 44,000. These three states comprised the 9th Civilian Defense region. There were 37,000 air raid wardens in California, 17,000 and 19,000, respectively, in Oregon and Washington. The imminence of a Japanese air raid was felt strongly by the local civilian defense corps. They responded by stepping up training programs and patrol operations. One of the most sensitive areas of concern were the schools. Civilian defense officials instituted air raid drills as a regular part of the school program. In San Francisco 19,000 elementary school children were issued identification tags stamped with their name and address, parents' name and phone, and serial number.

In every West Coast city, all outdoor activity such as concerts and sporting events was cancelled. For the first time in 23 years there was no Rose Bowl Parade or game in Southern California; no street celebrations were permitted on New Year's Eve. Instead, Durham, North Carolina was host site for the Rose Bowl game between Oregon State and the hometown Duke University. Blackouts were enforced with fines and jail sentences.

Americans were in a fight for their lives; our situation was hardly encouraging. After Pearl Harbor, the Japanese navy had the edge and authorities feared its forces might land a knockout blow before America was really prepared to fight. The sinking of merchant ships off the West Coast brought the war nearly to our front door.

Even more alarming, knowledgeable military and civilian leaders warned that America could **lose** the war—something the United States was unaccustomed to doing. Admiral William Standley, a member of the

Roberts' Commission on Pearl Harbor and later ambassador to the Soviet Union, said that "America through the West Coast can be brought to her knees." Attorney General Biddle cautioned San Francisco against underestimating the "evil strength" of our adversaries. Congressman Summers of Texas told the House, "We're being licked on the West Coast." Hanson W. Baldwin, military expert for the *New York Times,* wrote, "Our own errors are far more likely to determine our fate than anything Japan does." Finally, from the White House, came words to disturb every citizen on the West Coast. At a press conference, a reporter asked President Roosevelt whether he could guarantee that Japan would not attack Alaska or the Pacific Coast. The president could give no such assurance. The reporter then asked whether the U.S. Army and Navy were prepared to deal with anything? "Certainly not," Roosevelt replied. "Axis ships could shell San Francisco, Los Angeles and Seattle. Enemy bombers could bomb Sacramento tomorrow night." He had no comfort for the Pacific Coast.

Fifty-five thousand football fans jammed the stadium at Durham, N.C., for the 1942 Rose Bowl Game.
DUKE UNIVERSITY ARCHIVES

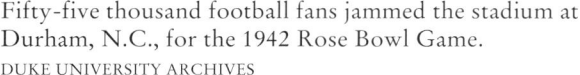

Auxiliary police with their white helmets and billy clubs are shown some weapons the enemy (Japanese) would likely use in an air raid.

Members of the Ulloa, Laguna Honda Boulevard, Idora Street and Sidney Way (ULIS) Club pose with their mobile units ready for bombing raids over San Francisco, August 1942.

Priests at a mountain retreat near the Bay Area take on their air watch duties.

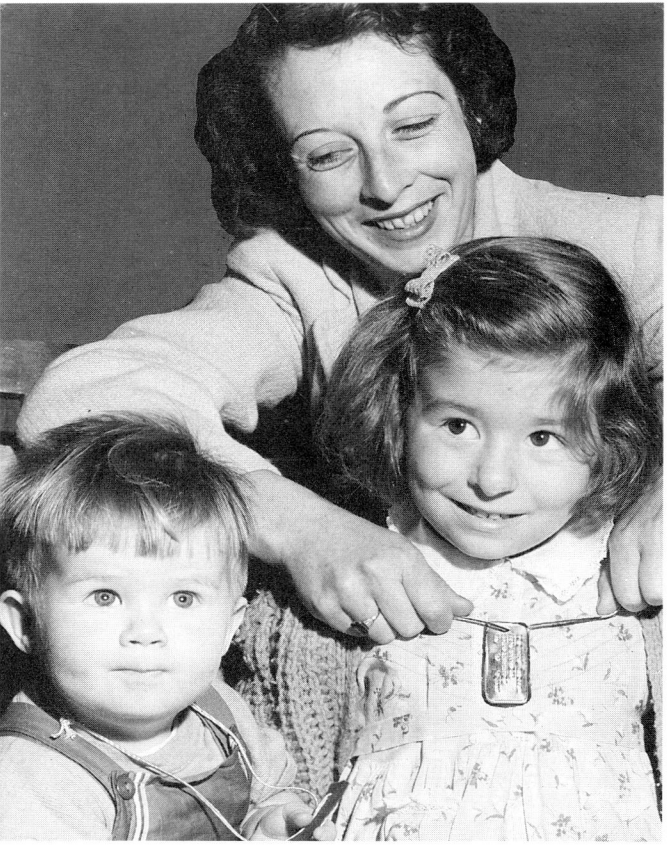

Nineteen thousand San Francisco children sported new metal identification tags following the first distribution at 12 elementary schools on Sept. 17, 1942. The tags bear the child's name, name of parents, address and telephone number, a serial number and in many cases, a religious preference.

The basement of city hall in San Francisco was the "nerve center" for the city's civilian defense. It was staffed 24 hours a day. A volunteer worker fills kerosene lanterns which would serve as auxiliary lighting in event of an emergency. Note the sand-bagged window in the background.

CHAPTER FIVE

Fear, Racism and Sadness

On Dec. 7, 1941, 127,000 persons who shared a common ancestry with the enemy lived within the continental United States. Of these, according to the 1940 census, 113,000 lived in the four Western states of Arizona, California, Oregon and Washington. About 94,000 were residents of California, or nearly three-fourths of the national total. Although loyal despite racial discrimination against them as cruel as any this nation has ever produced, they were all automatically considered guilty of sedition.

The first few days after Pearl Harbor found many Bay Area residents greatly alarmed by various reports, all false, that enemy aircraft carriers, battleships and submarines were offshore. With the Pacific fleet crippled, people felt they were vulnerable to a Japanese invasion at any moment, although knowledgeable military analysts already deciphering Japanese naval codes knew that full scale invasion was impossible.

War jitters weren't helped on Dec. 10 when an agent of the Treasury Department told army authorities and newspapermen that an estimated 20,000 Japanese in the San Francisco metropolitan area were "ready for organized action." Without checking the authenticity of the report, the Army's Ninth Corps Area staff hurriedly completed a plan for the evacuation of all Japanese-Americans, which was subsequently approved by the Corps area commander. The next morning, the Army called the local FBI chief who "scoffed at the whole affair as the wild imaginings of a discharged former FBI man." This stopped all further local action for the moment, but it added to wartime hysteria. Columnist Henry McLemore of the *San Francisco Examiner* summed it up best for many in the Bay Area when he wrote, "Herd 'em up, pack 'em off. Let 'em be pinched, hurt, hungry and dead up against it."

Soon, the anti-Asian racism that had plagued California for nearly a century boiled over. Harassed, assaulted, denied food, clothing, and jobs in their communities, many Japanese-Americans found themselves helpless. With mounting agitation for vigilante action against Asians, several state and federal officials warned Washington that unless adequate steps were taken, mob violence culminating in shootings and lynchings could be expected. By January 1942, property damage was taking place up and down the state.

On Feb. 19, with pressure for action against the Japanese-Americans growing, President Roosevelt signed Executive Order 9066, authorizing the Secretary of War to prescribe certain "military areas" and to exile "any or all" persons from them. Couched in broad language, the order was aimed at Japanese-Americans, although there were some 58,000 Italian and 22,000 German aliens in the Pacific states. In essence, Executive Order 9066 meant the imprisonment of the older, foreign-born Issei, their native-born offspring (the Nisei), and the Kibei, American citizens of Japanese ancestry who had spent their formative years in Japan and had returned to the United States. Swayed to sign such a document by the exaggerated claims of wartime necessity, a reluctant Roosevelt cautioned, "Be as reasonable as you can." [By racial decree, American citizens, stripped of their rights and property without hearings, were ordered evacuated from the Pacific Coast and interned east of the Sierras by April.]

Among those justifying the relocation were General DeWitt; Earl Warren, later Chief Justice of the United States (who was to advance his political career in California with speeches of fifth column activity among Japanese-Americans); and Justice William O. Douglas, who sanctioned the roundup for the U.S. Supreme Court. Surprisingly, one of the few high-ranking governmental officials arguing in support of the right of Japanese-Americans was FBI Director J. Edgar Hoover. He insisted that the majority would prove to be loyal citizens in the war with Japan. If there were spies and saboteurs in West Coast Japanese-American communities, military officials believed they would be found among the Kibei or resident aliens.

It is possible that hundreds of Japanese spies lived

along the Pacific Coast. Ken Ringle recalled that his father, Commander K.D. Ringle, a naval intelligence officer in 1942 directing counterespionage efforts on the West Coast, told him that he estimated the number of resident aliens to be less than three percent of the U.S. Japanese population, or 3,500 in the nation as a whole.[1] Commander Ringle, working out of a small office in the San Pedro YMCA, commanded five branch offices (one in San Francisco) and 75 men stretching from Sacramento to the Mexican border. In an atmosphere of growing suspicion, and betting on the absolute loyalty of the American-born Nisei, Ringle talked to Japanese-American farmers in the San Joaquin Valley, to community leaders, and to wharfside fishermen, telling them exactly who he was and his concern about Japanese spies. Sharing his worries about Japan's militarist ambitions, Japanese-American community leaders pointed out who were pro-American or militaristic Japanese. Furthermore, suspicious new arrivals were fingered. In fact, once when Ringle asked for help in identifying Los Angeles' militaristic Black Dragon Society, copies of the Society's complete rosters for the western half of the United States showed up in the mail.

Although an elaborate network of agents, codes, and contact-points did indeed exist, according to Ringle, it functioned out of the Japanese consulate in Los Angeles, with Itaru Tachibana, a Japanese naval officer as its head. When war broke out, most of the 450 known agents in Southern California were seized—including Toraichi Kono who once served as Charlie Chaplin's valet—and Japan's espionage system was eradicated. Captured documents revealed that Tachibana and Tokyo officials considered almost all of the resident aliens and American-born Japanese national traitors and not to be trusted. Significantly, not a single Japanese-American was ever brought to trial on charges of espionage or sabotage, either in the United States or Hawaii.

Prior to Pearl Harbor, a number of reports were re-

Lt. Gen. John L. DeWitt, commander of the 4th Army District. He carried out the evacuation of Japanese-Americans from the West Coast area.

ceived, not only by the Office of Naval Intelligence but by President Roosevelt himself, which unanimously agreed that in case of war, Japanese-Americans would "maintain a low profile (as they customarily do) and continue being productive, good citizens." Curtis B. Munson, who spent four months touring the West Coast as a special representative of the Department of Agriculture, told the President, "The Jap is an extremely good citizen and it is only because he is a stranger to us that we mistrust him."

In the Bay Area, with rumors spreading that internment was near, Issei and Nisei alike found themselves fired from their jobs, evicted from homes and farms, and attacked in the streets. California authorities revoked their licenses for markets, produce houses and stores. They were restricted from travel and commercial fishing; banks refused to cash Japanese-American

---

1. Ken Ringle, "What Did You Do Before the War, Dad?" *Washington Post*, Dec. 6, 1981.

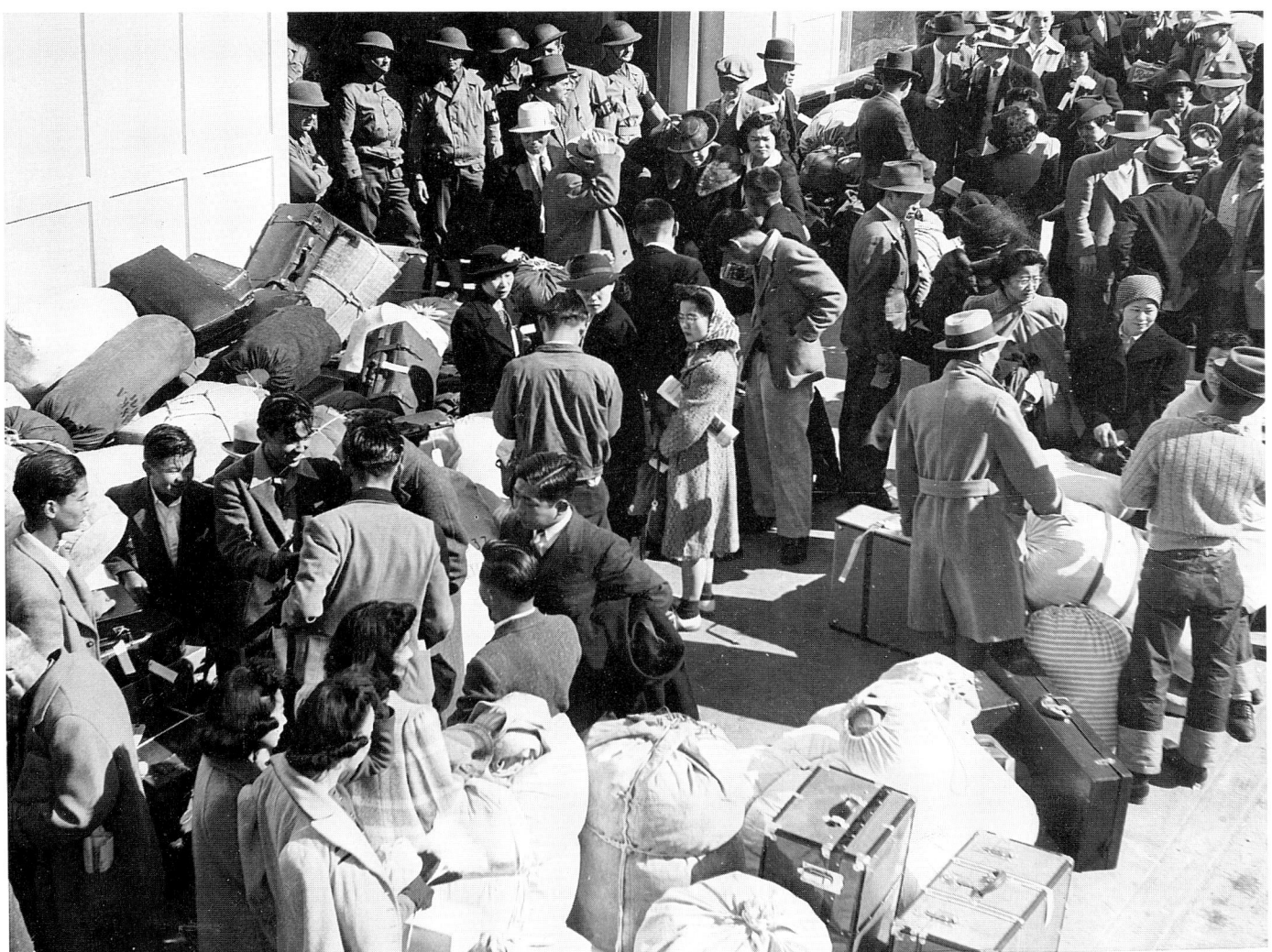

With military police standing in the background, part of the first 660 Japanese-Americans evacuated from San Francisco on April 6, 1942, mill around at a reception center. They were awaiting transportation to trains which took them to the Santa Anita Race Track in Los Angeles, a newly established assembly center.

checks; insurance companies cancelled their policies; milkmen and grocers refused to deliver or sell to them. Late in March, the roundup began. General DeWitt declared that if other methods failed, the Army would not shrink from using force to complete the evacuation. "A Jap's a Jap!" he declared. "It makes no difference whether he's an American or not." Some Japanese-Americans received as little as 48-hours' notice to dispose of their homes, businesses and farms. Of course, in the process, they fell prey to bargain hunters who bought their possessions for a fraction of their true value. Then, dragging baggage and bedrolls, these displaced Americans were carted off to wire-enclosed assembly centers of tar-paper barracks. In some instances, the structures were hastily converted fairgrounds or race tracks; many had to bed down in stalls reeking with manure.

Most went without protest, stoic in their belief that compliance would certify their loyalty to an America which was in essence dishonoring them. From these temporary centers, they would be shipped farther inland to 10 permanent camps in barren and isolated areas of Arkansas and the six Western states. For the duration of the war, they would live as prisoners in what President Roosevelt once referred to as "concentration camps."

The camps in which the internees suddenly found themselves often proved scenic spots of lonely loveliness. Confronted with the stark reality of barren frame "homes," dust-storms, and communal toilets with no partitions, the new arrivals had no choice but to adapt. Each family—sometimes two—was assigned to an "apartment"—one room measuring 20- by 25-feet in a wooden barracks. Although each camp quickly formed its own organizational schedules, rules and regulations, most maintained a similar pattern when it came to the routine of everyday life. For instance, residents were not allowed to leave the camps without special permission. During daylight hours, they could move within the centers, which often included several thousand acres. But after dark, they were confined to the residence area, usually a mile square and fenced with barbed wire.

"In Topaz (in central Utah)," recalled one Japanese-American, "it was the sickening smell of salt that first greeted you. And, you couldn't escape it or get used to it during the three years you were there." At Tule Lake (Newell, California), as well as Granada (Amache, Colorado), Poston (Colorado River, Arizona), Gila (Gila River, Arizona), Heart Mountain (Wyoming), and Manzanar (Inyo County, California), it was the dust and dirt, often blown by fierce winds. "Inside our houses, in the laundry, in the latrines, in the mess halls, dust and dirt. No matter where you went, you couldn't escape the dust," said another. Other War Relocation Authority (WRA) camps were Minidoka in southern Idaho and Rohwer and Jerome, both in southern Arkansas.

The WRA, headed by Milton Eisenhower, furnished the internees with food, lodging, medical care, and non-Japanese supervised education. Everyone was encouraged to work; the pay was $16 to $19 per month. Each worker was paid a cash allowance of $4.50 for clothing for members of his family. Everyone ate in communal dining halls and, although food was sufficient, it was not elaborate. Rationing restrictions were exactly like that followed by Americans on "the outside." Costing the WRA about 40 cents per day for food per person, menus included American and Japanese dishes, since the older generation favored rice, fish, tea, and leafy greens. By mid-1943, the evacuees, who upon their arrival tested and found the soil hard but potentially fertile, produced about one-third of their food requirements.

A reception center for Japanese-Americans was built on the infield of the Tanforan Race Track in the San Francisco area. On May 1, 1942, under the government exclusion order, 1,000 San Francisco Japanese-Americans were moved to this center.

In essence, the Japanese-Americans established a small-town existence in each camp, complete with fire, police, and post-office departments, schools, hospitals and camp newspapers. Every morning, most began their day by pledging allegiance to the American flag, although they had been imprisoned by their own government.

In spite of self-sustaining camps, each with its own democratic government, stores, workshops, beauty parlors, canteens, banks, and barbershops, life was lonely and hard. Japanese-Americans, known for their pride in rarely having been on welfare or locked up in prisons, were now wards of the government and guarded by armed soldiers. Fathers were no longer breadwinners, parents lost control of their children, and families rarely ate meals together. Changes in habits and values occurred overnight. Promising, productive lives had turned quadriplegic. The hopes and dreams from back home suddenly turned into a series of adaptations to unforeseen pressures and challenges. Although virtually all internees adjusted as time went on, many didn't, such as the several elderly who quietly hanged themselves in their rooms, or the young mother who crushed her infant and then committed suicide, or the man who placed his neck on a railroad track to be severed by a slow-moving freight. Confinement powerfully reinforced the pathos of their situation.

Many Japanese-Americans chose relocation to various parts of the United States, or joined the armed forces, rather than continue a life of immobility and dependence.

In July 1943, the WRA put in motion a program of permitting Nisei whose loyalty was beyond question to leave the relocation centers and live outside. Later, the same program was extended to aliens as well. Few evacuees took advantage of this program, because most of them had few contacts in the interior of the country that would result in jobs or other means of support.

Working with the War Manpower Commission, the U.S. Employment Service, the U.S. Department of Agriculture, and private groups and churches, WRA arranged for more than 10,000 Japanese-Americans to be placed in jobs outside the centers. Only those evacuees whose records had been checked and studied by the FBI and the WRA were permitted to leave.

Farm workers, farm operators, domestic servants, hotel and restaurant workers, and wives and sweethearts of Japanese-American soldiers leaving to join their husbands were the most numerous among the evacuees who left. The WRA placed many in war factories as lathe operators, foundry workers, drill-press operators, machine set-up men, welders, auto mechanics, draftsmen, and engineers.

In spite of all these contributions, some members of Congress and the State Department proposed legislation (unknown to Japanese-Americans) to strip all native-born Americans of Japanese ancestry of their citizenship and deport them to Japan after the war. A few elected officials went so far as to demand that the interned Japanese-Americans be used as reprisal targets for the mistreatment of American prisoners of war. One member of Congress even proposed a mandatory sterilization program.

Perhaps the ultimate form of indignity came in late February 1943, when all the internees 17 years or older were ordered to answer a questionnaire indicating their loyalty to the United States, as well as their willingness to served in the U.S. armed forces. Not only was the questionnaire insensitive to a people already denied their rights by being locked up for nearly a year, but the wording was confusing. Japanese nationals were asked in effect to render themselves stateless. Since they had been prohibited from becoming U.S. citizens all along, they were now asked to renounce the only citizenship they could have. For the Japanese-American citizens, they were asked to falsely incriminate themselves by "foreswearing" any allegiance to Japan, an allegiance they never had in the first place. Furthermore, women and the elderly were asked to serve on "combat duty whenever ordered." Despite the incongruity, ambivalence, and poor wording of the questionnaire, the majority of detainees signed the oath.

During 1943 and 1944, 33 percent of those interned, mostly young single men and women, were conditionally released on various forms of leaves or for military duty. On Jan. 28, 1943, Secretary of War Stimson announced a plan for the voluntary induction of Japanese-Americans into a separate combat unit with the statement that "it is the inherent right of every faithful citizen, regardless of ancestry, to bear arms in the nation's battle." President Roosevelt reiterated the same theme by declaring, "No loyal citizen of the United States should be denied the democratic right to exercise the responsibilities of his citizenship, regardless of his ancestry." Eventually, more than 8,000 would serve in the U.S. armed forces. And, despite suspicion and mistreatment by fellow servicemen, the young Nisei combat troops fought bravely in Italy and France. The Nisei 442nd Regimental Combat Team distinguished itself as the most decorated unit in World War II—18,000 citations. Only in the Tule Lake Internment Camp was there a persistent collective move-

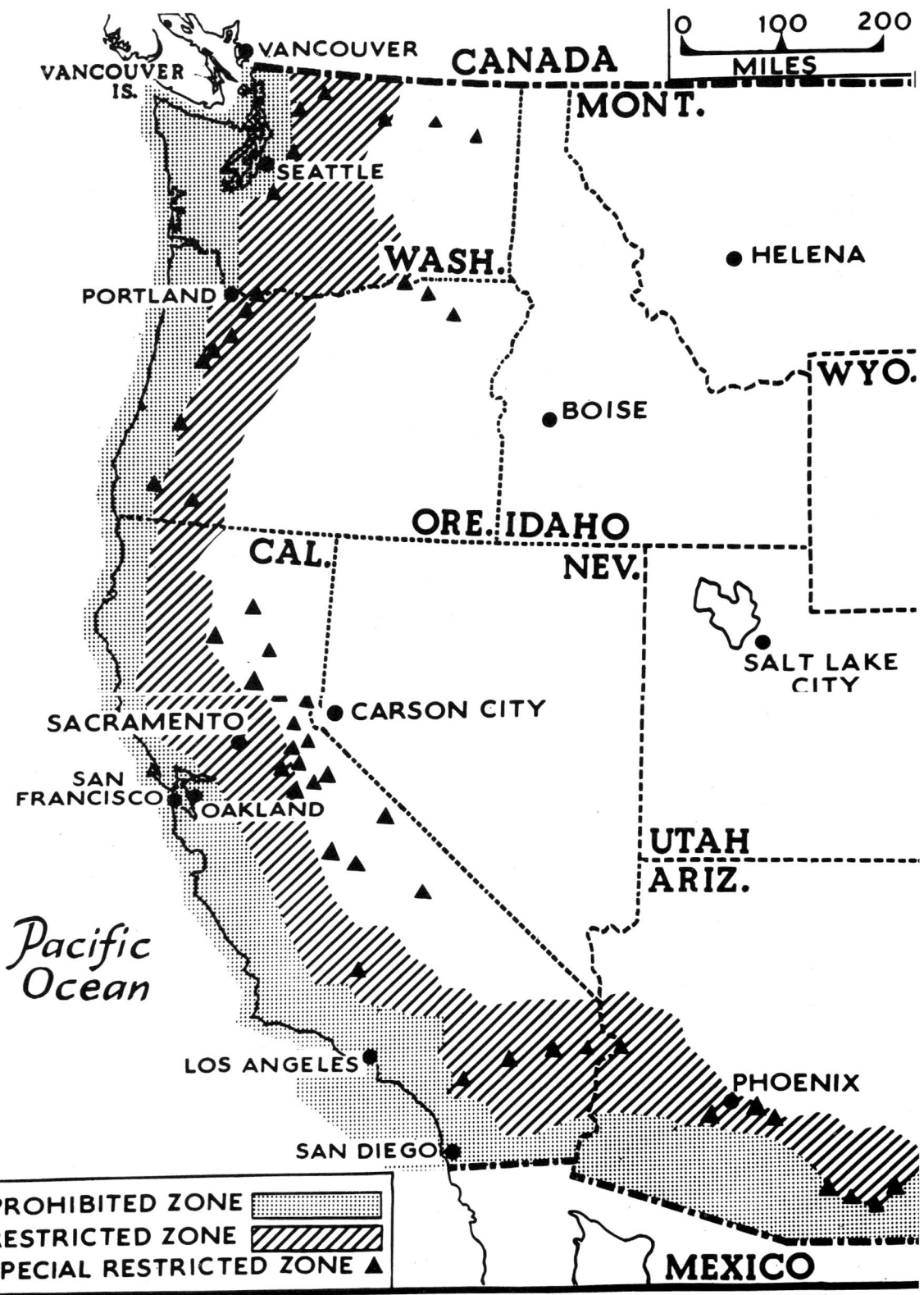

FACING PAGE: This March 3, 1942, map released by the government indicates areas of alien and Japanese-American exclusions. The dotted area along the coast excluded all enemy aliens and Japanese-Americans from residing there. The lined area allowed some Japanese-American residency, with restrictions imposed by the army. The black triangles denoted restricted areas such as armories, reservoirs and power stations. ABOVE: This map of Los Angeles put out over the AP network in March 1942 shows the extent of Japanese-American land held by lease near vital military and defense installations.

ment of noncooperation and resistance. This organized movement eventually stigmatized its residents as "disloyal" in the eyes of the American public and within a few months led to the camp's designation as a segregation center for evacuees whose loyalties were thought to be with Japan. The government itself admits, however, that what happened at Tule Lake was fostered by defective coordination between evacuee and administrative organizations; by a breakdown of communications between national and local representatives of the several branches of government responsible for registration; by the inability of project officials to clarify issues, procedures, and penalties for the evacuees; by rushing the program to meet predetermined deadlines; by government mistakes in the definition of penalties for noncooperation; and by use of armed force in the penalties.

By the end of the war, some 55,000 Japanese-American internees had taken up life outside the barbed wire. Those who eventually went back to their homes on the West Coast often found their property vandalized, their farms gone to seed, and their businesses bankrupt. Pressure groups were vocal in demanding that the Japanese-Americans be kept out permanently. Homes, farms and businesses left behind were occupied by whites unwilling to return property to rightful owners. Homes were burned and dynamited, and Japanese-Americans were targets of terrorist shootings.

In fact, more acts of violence and terrorism were committed against Japanese-Americans at the end of the war than at the beginning. Remains of Japanese-American soldiers killed in action overseas were refused burial in some hometown cemeteries. Many restaurants, hotels, barbershops, gas stations, and grocery stores refused to serve Japanese-Americans. Captain (and later U.S. Senator) Daniel K. Inouye, in full uniform with all his medals on, walked into a San Francisco barbershop, and was told, "We don't serve Japs here."

During their exile, the Japanese-Americans lost nearly half a billion dollars in assets—of which only about 10 percent were returned by a repentant federal government two decades later. The last mass detention camp did not close until October 1946. For some Japanese-Americans, reconstructing their lives was not easy. The elderly lost all they had worked for at the height of the productive years. None were able to save much for retirement. More than 20 percent were below poverty level by the 1970 census.

Men like Sam A. Hayakawa and Karl R. Bendetsen—the key figures in the War Relocation Authority who wrote the decree that anyone with one-sixteenth Japanese blood was to be interred as a public enemy—insisted that the camps weren't all that bad. Fortunately, the U.S. Commission on Wartime Relocation and Internment of Civilians, which in July 1981 began redress hearings into the wartime treatment of American citizens, thought otherwise. But redress is a small price to pay Americans for the cultural ignorance, racial hysteria, irrational paranoia and fear in part fostered by a government at its saturnine best.

Perhaps John Barrymore, the famed Hollywood actor of the 1920s and '30s, posed the best question. In March 1942, at the front gate of his Los Angeles mansion, Barrymore noticed his Japanese-American gardener, Kazuo Nishi, with his family and their few bundled belongings waiting to be carted away by soldiers. Dying of cancer with his mind fading in and out of reality, Barrymore couldn't understand why Nishi was leaving. When his daughter explained that America was now at war with Japan, Barrymore could only ask, "But is America at war with Nishi and his family?"[2]

---

2. Ron Bailey, *Homefront; USA*.

Police officers and FBI agents display some of the 69 cases of flares and high-powered fireworks seized on March 3, 1942, from the home of George Nakamura in Santa Cruz, California. Note that most of these boxes are marked "Made in Japan." There was no instance during the war of a resident Japanese-American committing an act of sabotage.

Among the nine Japanese detained when F.B.I. and local officers picked up 32 enemy aliens in widespread raiding in Vallejo adjacent to the Mare Island Navy Yard were Isekichi Matesuyama (left) and Mickiko Ebisu, laundry workers, shown being booked by Police Inspector Ralph Jensen. They were held "en route" to the U.S. attorney's office. Feb. 6, 1942.

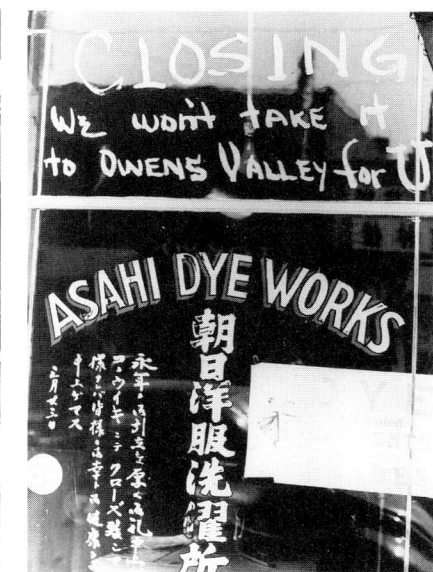

Top left: A roundup of enemy aliens occurred in Alameda County, California, in late February 1942. Some of these men were subsequently transported to an internment camp in North Dakota. Top right: No caption is necessary for this FDR Library photograph. Bottom left: Two Navy shore patrolmen stand guard in front of a Japanese-American owned newspaper office in San Francisco on December 8. Navy personnel were stationed in all sections of the city's Japanese settlement after the Pearl Harbor attack. Bottom right: A newsstand at the corner of 14th and Broadway in Oakland, Calif., on Feb. 27, 1942. On February 19, President Roosevelt delegated to the Secretary of War the power to exclude any person, alien or citizen, from any area that might be required, on the grounds of military necessity. This photo was taken by famous photographer Dorothea Lange.

In April 1942, these two San Francisco women and their children await evacuation while their husbands have already been rounded up as dangerous enemy aliens. Immediately after Pearl Harbor, FBI agents began rounding up hundreds of suspected agents of Japan, most of whom operated out of the Japanese Consulate in Los Angeles. Asked about the loyalty of Japanese-Americans, Lt. Gen. DeWitt replied, "A Jap is a Jap."

To demonstrate his loyalty on December 8, a Japanese-American placed a large sign reading, "I am an American" in his store window at 13th and Franklin streets in Oakland. The top sign, however, indicated he still had to get out. The owner, a University of California graduate, would soon be housed with thousands of other evacuees in a relocation camp.

Sometimes with as little as 48 hours' notice, Japanese-Americans were forced to close businesses, selling inventory for pennies on the dollar.
FDR LIBRARY

The forthcoming internment didn't dampen the enthusiasm of these fifth graders as they pledge allegiance at Raphael Weill Elementary School in San Francisco. Educational facilities would be provided for them in the camps by white teachers from nearby towns.

A billboard advertisement at the corner of Sutter and Octavia streets in San Francisco greeted more than 600 Japanese-Americans as they were evacuated to an assembly center in the war-jittery bay area during the first few months after America entered the war. Too few Americans were concerned about the personal rights of their Japanese-American neighbors.

All baggage was inspected before it was permitted in the Santa Anita Park Assembly Center in July 1942. FDR LIBRARY

The three Takeuchi sisters from Hayward, Calif., await the evacuation bus in May 1942. Evacuees were allowed to take only that which they could carry.

Ironing at the Pacific International Livestock Exposition Building in Portland, Oregon, May 1942.

Japanese-Americans from the Salinas, Calif., area await transportation to an assembly area. FDR LIBRARY

In Byron, Calif., laborers of Japanese ancestry return to their asparagus ranch after registration and interviews regarding their internment in three days. In spite of the eagerness of such men to be identified as Americans by their industry and responsibility, they were continually subjected to discrimination. White Californians had long been fearful of their growing numbers, their land purchases and the competition they posed in business.

Toshi Mizoguchi waits in a Byron, Calif., elementary school auditorium to register for evacuation in April 1942. He had arrived in California from Japan in 1892 and worked as a farm laborer on ranches and farms since that time. To demonstrate his allegiance to the United States, he is wearing an American flag printed on a celluloid button.

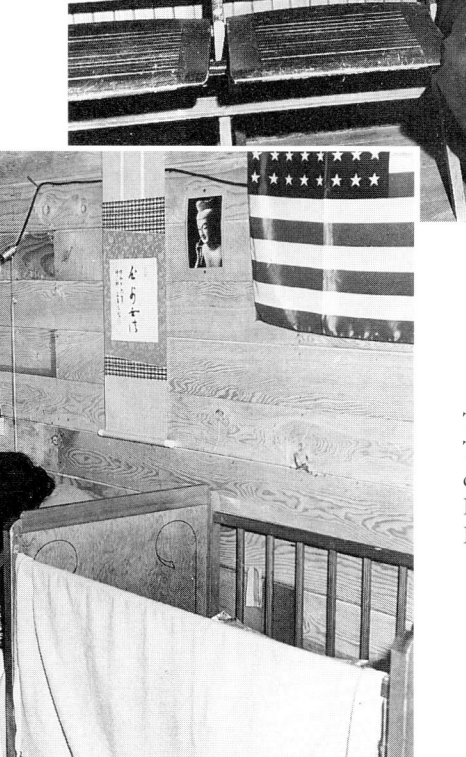

The five-person apartment of Rev. T. Terakawa, a Buddhist priest. Shown are his daughter, Hikoro and her friend, Lilian Hayashi at the Pacific International Livestock Exposition Building in Portland, Oregon.

THE WEST COAST GOES TO WAR 71

In Centerville, Calif., a grandfather awaits an evacuation bus. This photograph, taken by War Relocation Authority photographer Dorothea Lange in April 1942, symbolizes how Japanese-American hopes and dreams for the future were swept away overnight.

Evidence of the forthcoming evacuation of Japanese-Americans from the San Francisco area, April 1942.

The Wartime Civil Control Administration station at 2020 Van Ness Avenue in San Francisco on the morning of April 6, 1942, when the first group of 664 Japanese-Americans was evacuated from the city. Under Executive Order 9066, more than 112,000 Japanese-Americans would be removed to temporary relocation centers, then eventually shipped to 10 permanent camps in barren and isolated areas in the West and Arkansas.

Scene at departure time at the Los Angeles Santa Fe Railroad depot.

Among the first Japanese-Americans to be moved into the newly built assembly center at Tanforan Race Track, near San Francisco on April 28, 1942, were these who lined up at the rail—where once the railbirds watched the ponies run—and smiled. The group was among the 3,112 to be removed from restricted areas in the Bay area.

Office scene at the Visalia Control Section in April 1942. Signal Corps photographs such as this, showing smiling faces and the government's care and concern, were released for publication by the War Department's Bureau of Publication.

THE WEST COAST GOES TO WAR

At the Salinas Assembly Center while waiting a transfer to a relocation camp, a band of young students practice. Eighteen temporary assembly centers, hastily established on the West Coast in March 1942, were located at fairgrounds, race tracks and other public properties that provided utilities.

While a military policeman stands guard, Japanese-Americans watch the arrival of other evacuees to the Manzanar, Calif., Relocation Camp, April 2, 1942.

As two young boys play tag, a dust storm swirls around the desolate desert relocation camp at Manzanar, Calif. Located in Inyo County between Independence and Lone Pine, it was the home for 10,046 Japanese-Americans.

Various War and Navy department projects were carried out by the camp internees. Here women are busy constructing a camouflage net at Manzanar.

The irony of it all. A mother of Japanese ancestry in Florin, Calif., is shown picking strawberries in a field a few days before evacuation. Her soldier son, granted leave to assist his family in evacuating, is shown beside her. The Japanese-Americans working in this community were dependent on their returned servicemen for the errands—shopping, banking, etc.—since they were the only ones permitted to travel into town nine miles away.

BELOW: The Tule Lake Relocation Camp at Newell, Calif. TOP RIGHT: Prefabricated structures awaited the new arrivals at Tule Lake. Despite the temporary nature of this and similar communities, Japanese-Americans tried to make them homelike. Within several weeks after the first newcomers arrived, neat rows of radishes, carrots, and beets began growing. Flowers miraculously appeared in window boxes. Tables, chairs and vanity sets—fashioned from scraps of lumber—soon furnished the bare apartments. BELOW RIGHT: Every structure—residences, schools, cafeterias, and recreation halls—at the Tule Lake Center was identical with these shown here. On the right is the camp's "co-op" store. At left is a bank and newspaper/magazine store, with a barber and beauty shop in the rear.

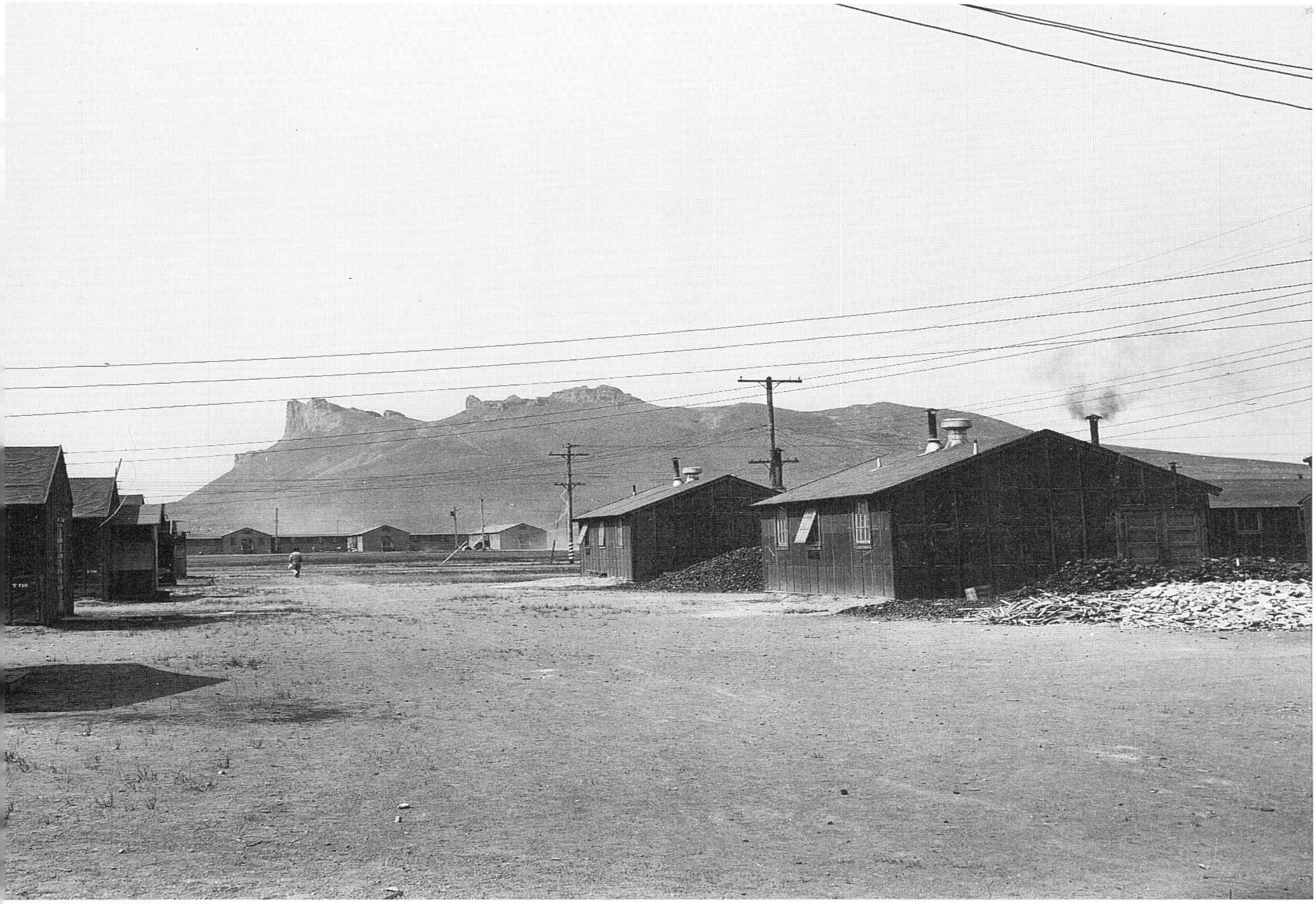

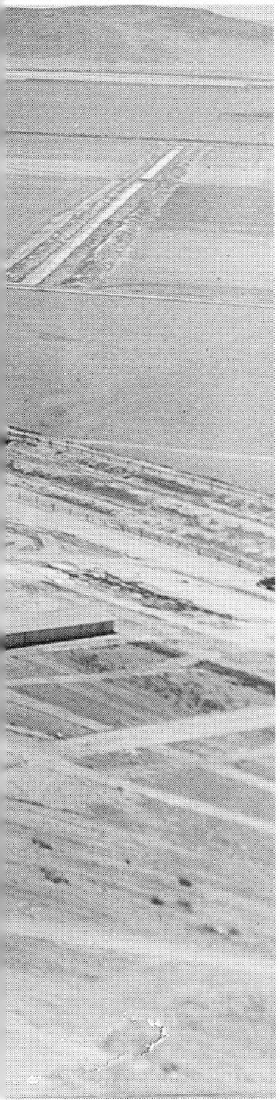

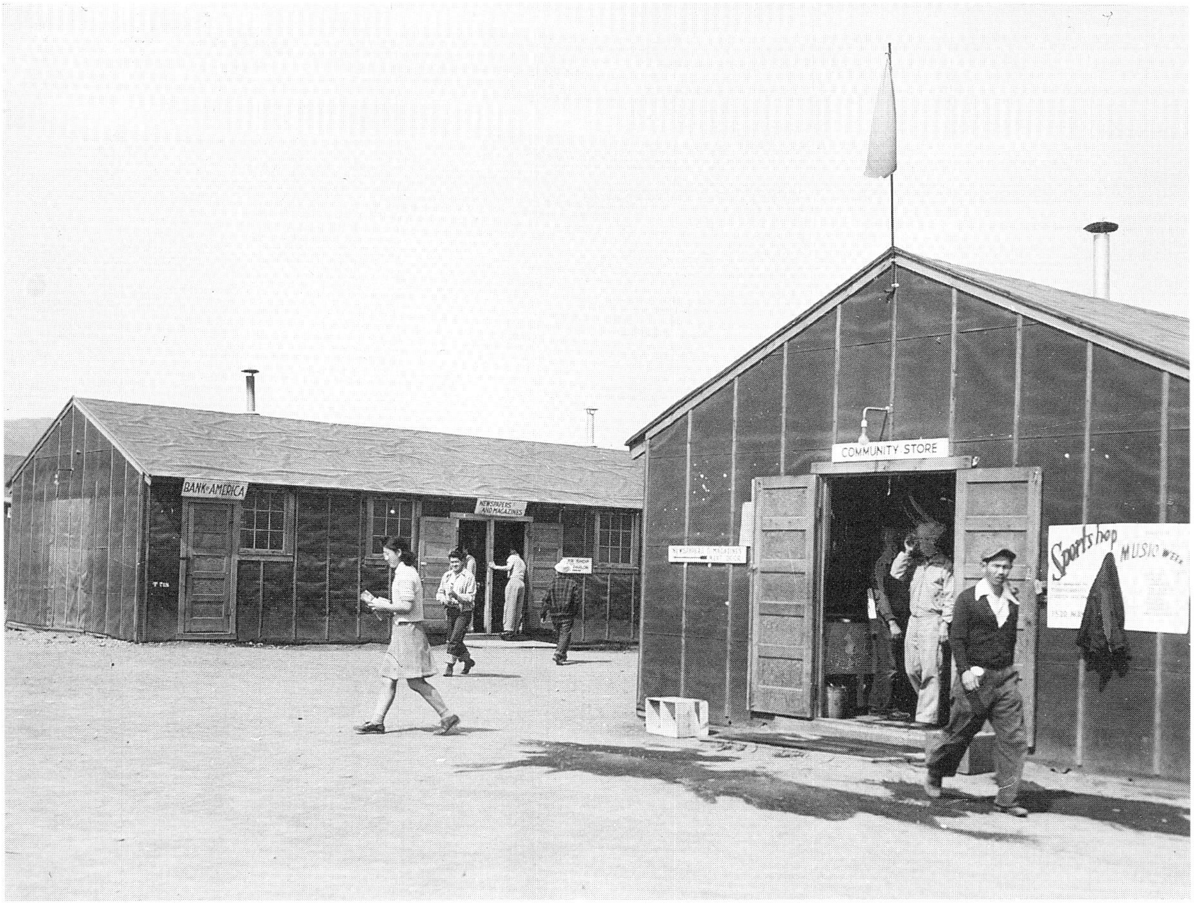

The Tule Lake Bank of America. The evacuees were supplied with food, housing, hospitalization, medical and dental care and necessary clothing. During their temporary residence in the Assembly Centers, they were given nominal allowances for incidentals. Upon application, the evacuees were given secure coupon books, which could be used for the purchase of merchandise at the center exchanges or stores. These books entitled a single adult to $2.50 of goods per month, a couple to $4.00, an individual under 16 to $1.00. The maximum allowance for any family was $7.50 per month.

BELOW: Whenever a member of the armed forces, or famed 442nd Regimental Combat Team, returned home to visit family and friends, it was worthy of the news media taking pictures. Milton S. Eisenhower, Director of the War Relocation Authority, publicized the growing contributions made to the war effort by Nisei volunteers. Said Eisenhower, "Just because these people are Japanese there is no reason why they should not be treated decently and humanely by white Americans, who have a heavy obligation to be tolerant."

CHAPTER SIX

The West Coast Rolls Up Its Sleeves

DURING THE WEEKS following Pearl Harbor, the West Coast buckled down to the immense tasks of arming itself to defend against possible invasion and supplying the military forces with the tools to win the war. The potential of the United States armed forces had yet to be realized. But one thing was certain: The attack on Pearl Harbor resulted in mobilization of manpower and industry unprecedented in American history.

President Roosevelt immediately hastened the nation's military and economic preparations for war. Declaring Jan. 1, 1942, a national day of prayer, he said, "The new year of 1942 calls for courage and the resolution of old and young to help win a world struggle in order that we may preserve all we hold dear." By mid-January the President had launched a massive production program, adding, "Let no man say it cannot be done." For 1942, U.S. industry was asked to produce 50,000 to 60,000 airplanes, 45,000 tanks, 20,000 antiaircraft guns, and eight million deadweight tons of merchant ships. Most of the airplanes and ships would come from factories on the West Coast. During the first seven months of the European war, from Sept. 1, 1939, to March 31, 1940, American factories completed and delivered to the United States Army and Navy 477 planes; to Great Britain, 311; and to France, 459; for a total of 1,247 at an average of 178 deliveries per month. In the Fall of 1941 average production was to reach about 550 planes per month for a yearly total of 6,600. The gap between these figures and the President's goal of 50,000 planes per year was staggering. German production was estimated to be 6,000 planes per month.

Few Americans doubted that the goal could be achieved, and aircraft manufacturers were jubilant. As it turned out, 47,653 military airplanes were produced in 1942. This was over two and one-half times the production of 1941 but still below the President's goal. Numerous difficulties impeded the 1942 program. Deliveries of machine tools were insufficient, shortages of many parts and accessories occurred and shortages of the more critical components limited the output of finished planes. The output of raw materials for airplane production increased, but bottlenecks were encountered securing some fabricated materials, particularly aluminum and alloy steel forgings.

Military authorities were concerned about the vulnerability of West Coast aircraft plants. In Seattle, Boeing was located between two bodies of water and clearly definable landmarks. Simple triangulation or compass headings could easily direct enemy aircraft to the target. Approximately $3 million was spent on Boeing Field and at Plant 2 for bomb shelters, machine gun platforms, troop dormitories, casualty stations, and a message center. Plant camouflage installation costs totaled an additional $1 million.

The roof of Plant 2 had the most elaborate camouflage. It was made to resemble a 26-acre village and included chicken-feather trees, painted canvas buildings, and burlap lawns landscaped with shrubs of spun glass on wire. The village had 53 residences, 24 garages, a corner service station, a neighborhood store, and three greenhouses. All told, there were 42,000 square yards of dummy streets and 85,000 yards of camouflage texturing. The village neighbors, Boeing Field and Beacon Hill, merged with the new landscape. Fake roads appeared to run down Beacon Hill, across the field, and into the rooftop village. Simulated cars were parked on the streets, and clothes could be seen on clothes lines. Hedges and truck-garden crops were painted with cold water paint, and the colors changed with the seasons. Straggling lanes and country roads obliterated the runways. All this construction was to make the Boeing location appear further south of the city, and it passed all aerial tests. So complete was the total effect that pilots flying at more than 5,000 feet often reported difficulty getting their bearings.

In California, life was also changed but that didn't stop an influx of new residents. In 1940, tourists spent more than $202 million in Southern California, and one out of every 10 newcomers to the state settled there, most in Los Angeles. More and more Americans were discovering the area and its pleasant climate and were moving there. Pearl Harbor was at first a serious blow to tourism, since rumors circulated that the government had declared Southern California "unsafe." The chambers of commerce went out of their way to advertise that travel conditions were normal, and that only 11 of 300 winter vacation events had been cancelled because of the war. The Los Angeles Chamber of Commerce beguiled the hundreds of thousands of servicemen swarming through the area. The uniformed tourists were spending a good deal of money in the city. Besides the organized tour of the movie stars' homes and other peacetime attractions, soldiers could now visit the famous Hollywood Canteen, where Hedy Lamarr or Betty Grable might pour them a cup of coffee and serve them a doughnut.

But the main event for Southern Californians occurred on the production lines. One-fifth of all government aircraft contracts in 1941 and 1942 went to Southern California plants, which produced more planes than any other state. In fact, without their production, the country could not have waged an effective war in the air. Actually, Southern California had a head start on the rest of the nation. Its aircraft factories were already producing in wartime quantities before plant conversion elsewhere was much more than an idea on a blueprint. They had acquired practice, know-how, and a large backlog of orders.

Southern California had shifted noticeably and economically in relation to its great movie studios. It was no longer devoted slavishly to Hollywood. By the Fall of 1942, the important places were Burbank, Long Beach, Inglewood, Santa Monica, and San Diego, where the huge and still-growing aircraft plants were located. Los Angeles, which the year before seemed a mere appendage of its own suburb of Hollywood, was now asserting itself and its industrial importance. Youngsters in the streets who once knew every movie star by the look of their automobiles no longer cared so much about the stars. Instead they were identifying P-38s, B-25s, and A-20s buzzing overhead. Sunday drivers were now more interested in going out to look at the aircraft plants than in passing in front of the homes of movie stars.

Aircraft production was the biggest industry. The 40-mile radius around Los Angeles contained the thickest concentration of airplane factories in the United States. Here Douglas made its A-20 attack bombers and the military versions of the DC-3 transports. Lockheed made P-38 fighters, North American made the B-25 bombers and the P-51 fighter, and in San Diego, Consolidated produced the B-24 bomber and the PBY flying boat.

There was more than just aircraft in the new industrial Southern California. Its shipyards held building contracts worth $600 million. New steel and aluminum mills were being built. Half a billion dollars was being spent on a variety of other war goods. California was still the third largest agricultural state in the union, and the southern part of the state grew most of the crops. Southern California was also one of the three most important oil-producing regions in the nation. The southern portions of Los Angeles were covered with oil derricks.

With all this the changes usually accompanying industrialization were not much in evidence. There was little smoke, grime and congestion. Fontana's new steel mill was surrounded by orchards instead of the customary steel-town concentration of drab houses. Only at night were any signs of industrial activity visible. At sundown the lights of the shipyards and outdoor airplane assembly lines gleamed brightly, and restless sleepers could hear the dull roar of airplane motors being warmed up and tested in the newly finished planes.

The workers came from all over. The once neglected and unwanted migrant farmhands were eagerly sought by expanding industries. A motto of the time was, "Come on you Okies and Arkies, let's take on Japan. We took California without losing a man." The movie studios lost a few steady workers to the war plants, and the periphery of the film industry moved into war work. Men and women who had come to Hollywood to land a job in the movies found that they were needed in the war industries. The shipyards on Terminal Island had enough musicians employed to form two full-fledged orchestras.

The war workers were mostly young, but there was a significant population of people over 50 who had retired in the California sunshine and now decided to pitch in and help. Most were untrained but intelligent enough to learn simple skills quickly. Being new to the job, these workers generally had a brisk amateur enthusiasm that responded to production quotas and the need for speed.

All the aircraft industries cooperated, loaning each other engineers, materials, machines, and even ideas. The Aircraft War Production Council, whose members were the large airplane companies and whose top management met once every month, coordinated the exchange. Engineers visited each other's factories to observe working methods. When Douglas needed some metal heat-treated in a hurry, Northrup pitched in and did it. When North American ran short of landing gear struts, it bought some that Douglas did not immediately need. In a single month the Council's work had prevented or broken up more than 1,800 bottlenecks in an industry where any setback, great or small, could be a matter of life or death.

Cooperation and showmanship kept production up and workers happy. Most of the aircraft plants were unionized, and the management was on familiar and usually friendly terms with union leaders. No grave jurisdictional disputes among unions arose; no serious strikes occurred in the aircraft industry except one unauthorized sit-down strike at North American. There was a fine air of Hollywood razzle-dazzle in management-employee relations. During lunch periods and after work, employees had free entertainment. Whenever a company's airplanes did well in battle, bulletins and congratulatory letters were announced company-wide. There was great pride in being associated with a winning effort.

All along the West Coast the war had a healing effect on the labor strife that had been so prevalent in the past. Perhaps the most significant change, almost overnight, was the new stature of Harry Bridges of the Longshoremen's Union and Dave Beck of the Teamsters. The two became patriots, frowning on strikes and urging their fellow workers to put forth greater effort. San Francisco led the nation in organizing a Unity for Victory Committee, uniting all labor in the common cause. Anyone who knew the history of Harry Bridges would have been astounded to find him urging a union speed up, or to hear San Francisco employers referring to him as a labor statesman. Ancient labor foes such as Roger D. Lapham, chairman of

Henry J. Kaiser inspects his shipyards at Richmond, California, in 1943.

the American-Hawaiian Steamship Company and in 1942 a member of the National War Labor Board, said, "Harry is one of the June boys," referring to one who suddenly turned interventionist when Germany invaded Russia in June 1941. But Lapham acknowledged Bridges' efforts in forcing the organization of many employers associations that did so much to stabilize labor relations in the city during these urgent times.

The influx of defense workers posed the dilemma of housing an increasing population. In Los Angeles the population spread over the landscape, and the automobile was virtually the only way to get to work because the city lacked municipal transportation. Industry forged a unique plan to cut employees' travel time by swapping workers, assigning them to plants nearest their homes.

The success of the West Coast's wartime industrial achievements was largely a collective effort—the determination of assembly-line workers, labor unions, industrial managers, and many others. But certain individual efforts stand out, and none more than the work of Henry J. Kaiser. "Old Henry," as the newspapers and radio comedians called him, founded his first

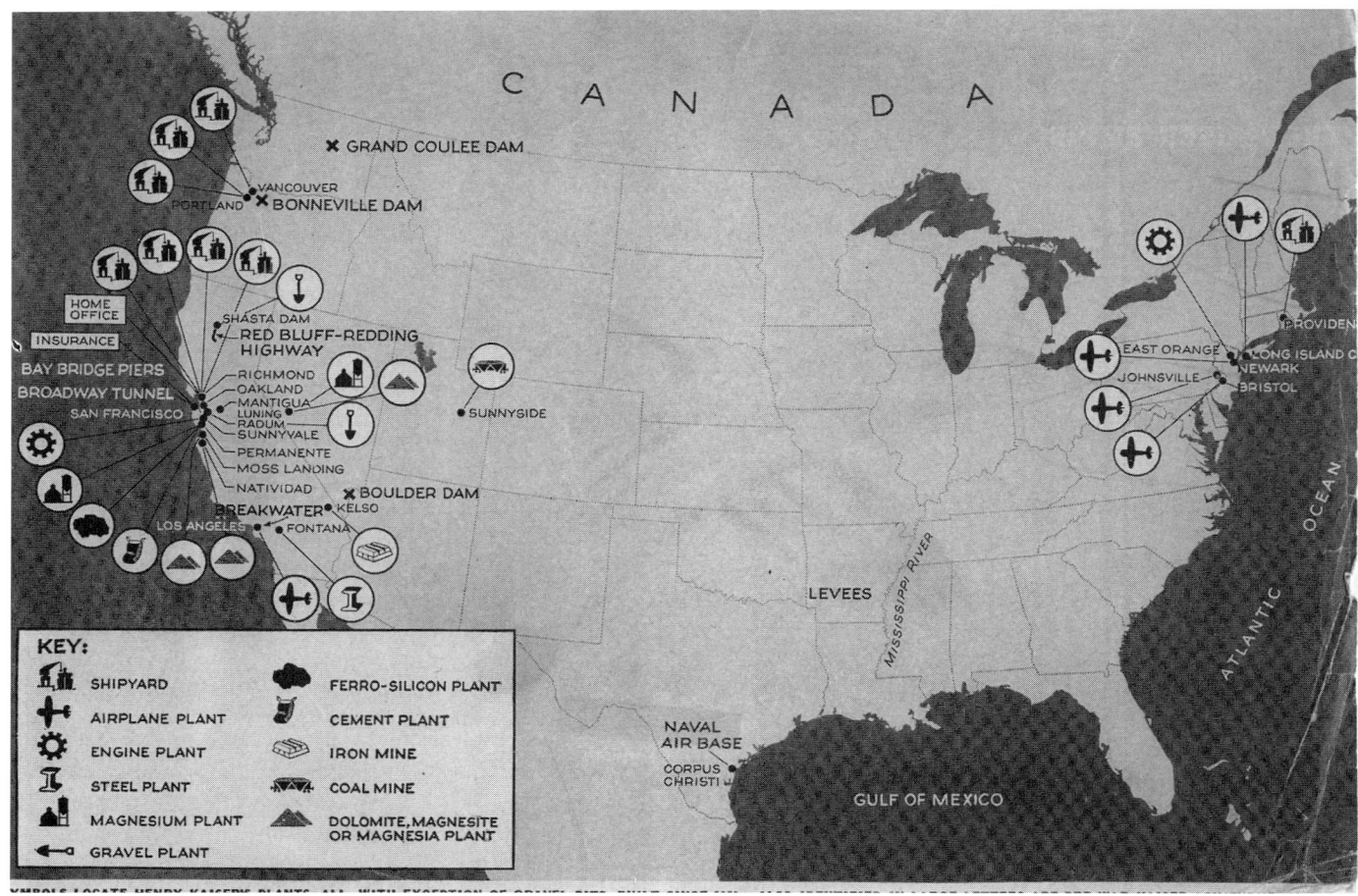

Map showing Kaiser's plants throughout the country, built since 1939. Large letters are pre-war Kaiser projects. PHOTO AT RIGHT: The *S.S. Samuel Adams* gets ready to slide down the ways at the California Shipbuilding Corporation Yard in Long Beach, Jan. 31, 1942.

company, the Henry J. Kaiser Company, Ltd., in Spokane, Washington, in 1914, and from that time on, he was never outdone.

In 1921 he moved his company to Oakland, California, and by the late 1930s, his associated corporations were involved in more than 1,000 projects. By the end of the war, his contributions to national defense would include a massive shipbuilding yard in Richmond, California, the largest artillery shell factory in the United States, the Kaiser Permanente magnesium plants, a sizeable bulk cement plant, and a steel mill in Fontana, California.

Kaiser's reputation was built not only on the size of his industrial empire, but on his remarkable ability for getting things done. And he got nothing done better than in his Richmond shipyards where he built the famous "Liberty" class merchant ships that became the lifeline of supply for Allied armies on all fronts.

Using prefabricated sections—a revolutionary idea in shipbuilding—the Kaiser shipyard turned out its first Liberty ship (the *Robert E. Peary*) in the amazing time of four days and 15 hours. Kaiser's industrial genius was widely imitated—old Henry was never reluctant about sharing his ideas—and by the second year of the war the Liberty ships had redressed the balance of Allied shipping.

Despite the industrial boom, the West Coast had a serious problem on its hands: a shortage of farm laborers to harvest annual agricultural products worth $1 billion. Much of the product was perishable specialty crops that had to be harvested in large quantities at exactly the right time. During the Spring of 1942 the farmers of California's rich San Joaquin Valley had to plow under sugar beets and watch helplessly while cherries ripened and rotted on the trees. In this valley, which long had known the evil social effects of a surplus labor supply and where much of the nation's fruits and vegetables were raised, American-born farm hands were volunteering for the armed forces. Filipino farm workers were hustled off to coastal shipyards. Japanese farms had already been uprooted. Even the once unwelcome Arkies and Okies and their sons joined the rush to the military and war production jobs. Despite the high wages to harvest sugar beets ($20 per

day) and pick cherries (60 cents per pail), few workers were available. Consequently, by July 1942 a quarter of the San Joaquin Valley's harvest was lost. In Salinas, from which 25,000 carloads of lettuce were shipped around the nation each year (one-half of the nation's supply), only 1,000 of the normal 3,000 Filipino laborers were on hand to do the job. A frantic call to the state employment office in Los Angeles for 1,000 Mexican-American workers brought a promise of 36 and the actual arrival of 12. The crisis was to grow more serious all along the coast, reaching a peak with the August-October season for peaches, grapes, and tomatoes. Workers were eventually brought in from Mexico to do the job.

West Coast industry reacted quickly and with an amazingly single-minded determination after Pearl Harbor. Winston Churchill had called America the "Arsenal of Democracy," but on Dec. 7, 1942, the phrase was just that—only a phrase. To help make it a reality to match and then overwhelmingly surpass the Axis war industries, the West Coast rolled up its sleeves and got to work.

Kaiser's Liberty ships supplied Allied combat fronts from Pacific atolls to the frozen harbor of Murmansk in Russia. Boeing's B-17s would command the European skies—and its B-29s would carry the weapon that would end the war. North American's B-25 Mitchell bombers would be flown by James Doolittle's Tokyo raiders. And the West Coast's fertile soil would help supply food for men at arms and civilians at work.

The West Coast, like Old Henry, got the job done.

This remarkable series of photographs shows how Kaiser's Oregon Shipbuilding Corporation Yard in Portland cut 14 days from the record of his Richmond Permanente Yard No. 2 by launching a 10,500-ton freighter 10 days after work started.

FIRST MORNING
Ship's bottom rapidly shaped

SEVENTH AFTERNOON
On "home stretch"

THIRD AFTERNOON
Bulkheads in place

FIFTH MORNING
Deck rushed

NINTH MORNING
Superstructure in place

TENTH DAY
Ready for launching

Kaiser's Richmond shipbuilding facility operated around-the-clock with workers building Liberty ships.

Top photo: The M/S *Brevard* at the Richmond, Calif., shipyards in the Bay Area.

Bottom photo: Although three ships were launched earlier on May 22, 1942, at Portland's Oregon Shipbuilding Corporation, this was the scene at midnight of the same day as work progressed on more ships.

Close-up views of the fake town built on top of the Boeing Aircraft factory in Seattle. From an aerial view this would appear to be an ordinary American town.

THE WEST COAST GOES TO WAR 89

ABOVE: Sign at the Boeing Aircraft Plant in Seattle, October 1941. BELOW: B-17 heavy bombers line up at Boeing's assembly plant. The photo was apparently taken during a shift change.

90   THE WEST COAST GOES TO WAR

Mare Island, in the Bay area, was one of the most important defense facilities on the West Coast.

Inspecting rifle shells in San Francisco.

A woman worker at Boeing operates a Rockwell hardness tester. America's main heavy bomber, the B-17 "Flying Fortress" was developed and built at the Seattle plants of Boeing.

Workers at the Richmond shipyards took a personal interest in directing the rubber floor mats from their cars to Axis leaders as essential parts of future American bombers. These workers and thousands of others who contributed their floor mats felt that donating scrap rubber was just as important as building ships.

These "Rosie The Riveters" show that a woman's place was no longer solely in the home. They worked at the Moore Shipyard in Oakland, Calif., 1942.

AT RIGHT: The Naval Drydocks at Hunters Point at the Mare Island Navy Yard.

BELOW: Submarine base at Mare Island Navy Yard.

ABOVE: Aerial view of the outer harbor area and the Oakland Army Base, California, mid-1942.

AT RIGHT: The Oakland Naval Supply Center in January 1942, just a few weeks after it was officially commissioned.

AT LEFT: Thousands of huge ship ventilators form this weird pattern of war production in the Los Angeles plant of the Weber Showcase and Fixture Company.

BELOW: Trailer City on the outskirts of Vallejo, California. The government had to build trailer courts like this throughout the country to house the thousands of defense workers moving to the cities.

Top photo: Scrap metal drive on Valley Street in San Francisco, 1943. Bottom photo: Students of Fairmont Grammar School in San Francisco flash the V for Victory sign from a pile of scrap they have collected.

Left: Tin was another essential war item in great demand by the military.

Bottom: One of the major salvage items during the war was old tires and other rubber products. The main supply of natural rubber was reduced considerably during the war and the demand from the military was greatly increased.

High school students in Alameda County, Calif., helped in the farm fields due to the shortage of workers.

Inset: More scrap collected by San Francisco school children.

A bird's-eye view of a portion of the Laguna Honda Community Victory Gardens in San Francisco. These gardens, situated on a slope of the 7th Avenue side of Laguna Honda Home, consisted of 300 families. Sponsored by the Victory Garden Advisory Council and under the jurisdiction of San Francisco Junior College, the project was judged by Federal officials on a nationwide tour of Community Victory Gardens as the "best planned and most beautiful community project" in the nation. Twin Peaks and the Laguna Honda Home are in the background, 1943.

Armed with garden tools, this junior victory garden army paraded every day from the Canon Kip Community House to a plot near Eighth and Howard streets in San Francisco to work their vegetable plots.

CHAPTER SEVEN

Shangri-La and Midway: The End of the Beginning

TIME MAGAZINE called them the worst weeks of the war. In mid-February 1942, news from the fronts, home and abroad, was so bad, *Time* editorialized, as to rival the dark days of 1864 when "the fate of the nation was in the balance." German submarines, operating in "Wolfpacks," were sinking an average of three ships per day in the North Atlantic, often—to add insult to injury—within hailing distance of the American East Coast. The ocean liner *Normandie*, impounded from Vichy France and scheduled to be converted into an aircraft carrier, blew up in her New York harbor berth—allegedly the work of fifth columnists. The German army poised for a Spring offensive against Russia.

News from the Pacific was equally disheartening. Singapore, the lynch-pin of Southeast Asia, had fallen; the Japanese, avoiding the heavy British naval guns aimed permanently to sea, overwhelmed the colony's defenses from the rear. Farther to the east, in the Philippines, a determined Japanese army drove an equally determined—but hopelessly outnumbered and undersupplied—American army into the Bataan Peninsula and eventual capitulation. Was it possible that we could **lose** the war?

In mid-February it certainly seemed possible, especially to those on the West Coast, where the war was closer to a civilian population already unnerved by blackouts and enemy submarines. But the war came closer even.

It was a holiday—Washington's birthday—and that evening at 7:00, many Southern Californians had just cleared the dinner dishes and tuned in station KFI in Los Angeles to listen to one of President Roosevelt's "fireside" chats. "My friends ...Washington's birthday is an appropriate time for us to talk with each other about things as they are today and things as we know they shall be," the President said. As he spoke the Japanese submarine *I-17* surfaced a few miles north of Santa Barbara, California. Aircraft spotters and motorists on U.S. Highway 101, believing the submarine to be an American vessel, watched as the *I-17* cruised northward and then turned to the east.

At 7:05, the *I-17* was abreast of Santa Barbara and the Barnsdall oil field in Ellwood, six miles to the west. Koso Nishino, the submarine commander, ordered his deck gun loaded, locked, then fired, and the shell screamed over the oil plant to explode harmlessly into a hillside nearly a mile inland. For nearly 45 minutes the *I-17* steamed abreast of the oil plants and storage facilities in Ellwood and Goleta, firing as many as 29 rounds at the California coast. At 7:45 the submarine turned and steamed away on the surface.

The next morning, as curiosity seekers clogged Highway 101, Santa Barbara assessed the damage: $500. Shrapnel had punched several holes in the oil company's sheds, but beyond that, the damage was negligible. Most of the shells landed off-target, and many were duds that plowed harmlessly into the ground. But the psychic damage to West Coast war nerves was far greater—so great that later in the week, on the morning of Feb. 25, more than 1,400 rounds of antiaircraft shells were fired from Los Angeles at phantom airplanes, in zealous defense, if not perhaps in sheer frustration.

THE BATTLE OF LOS ANGELES: THE NIGHT OF "WHO FLEW?"

IN INGLEWOOD, Maureen Platt thought it was the water heater. Somehow the tank must have emptied, she thought, and the overheated metal jacket was expanding, emitting popping and cracking noises that sounded like machine gun fire. Soon it would explode and demolish the small Kelso Avenue apartment she shared

The oil derricks west of Santa Barbara at Goleta and the Ellwood Refinery—scene of the first enemy attack on U.S. soil since the War of 1812.

A long-range Japanese *I*-class submarine such as this lobbed 25 shells from its deck guns into the oil fields at Goleta.

with her newborn son and husband Larry, a defense worker at the nearby North American Aviation plant. When the couple stumbled groggily into the kitchen shortly before 3:00 on the morning of Feb. 25, 1942, to check the malfunctioning water heater, they found it hissing and gurgling smoothly. The popping and cracking sounds, which had by now become a thumping noise, came not from the kitchen but from *outside* the apartment. Opening the windows, the couple was astonished to see the sky above Los Angeles ablaze with searchlights, 50-caliber antiaircraft tracer bullets, and the brilliant yellow flash of exploding antiaircraft shells. The Battle of Los Angeles was joined.

A few miles to the northeast, at 78th Street and Western Avenue in south central Los Angeles, the noise was positively fearful. Ten-year-old Bill Weller tumbled out of bed and joined his mother, brothers, and neighbors in nightclothes and slippers in front of their houses. Antiaircraft batteries only a block away at Manchester and Western were firing at what young Weller believed to be "planes in a V-formation heading north toward Burbank."

Weller's father, Bill Sr., was 21 blocks away, working the night shift at the Hostess Baking Company. Minutes before the Los Angeles skies erupted, civilian defense officials had warned the bakery of an alert, and the night shift was ordered to turn off all lights. Weller then joined his fellow bakers to watch the spectacle from the street. He saw no planes but did see "a huge orange and red fireball in the sky" that quickly fell to the ground. The bakers, deciding their white uniforms would make perfect targets for Japanese aviators, retreated to the darkened bakery.

Just as everyone who remembers Pearl Harbor also remembers where they were or what they were doing when they heard the news on Dec. 7, so do Angelinos recall similar details of the night of "Who Flew?" Some recollections, like Maureen Platt's, are humorous; some, like young Bill Weller's, are no doubt erroneous; and some, like Bill Weller Sr.'s, are downright puzzling. One woman recalled that "huge spotlights were on one plane and—oh my!—the artillery guns were really shooting."[1] A Los Angeles air raid warden saw not one but 10 flights of enemy planes "forming a perfect V, like a flight of wild geese flying very high."[2] In the Tarzana Hills, some residents claimed to have seen a mysterious string of red lights "in a V-form pointing toward the Lockheed aircraft plant" in Burbank.[3] A

---
1. Bert Webber, *Retaliation: Japanese Attacks and Allied Countermeasures on the Pacific Coast in World War II* (Corvallis: Oregon State University Press, 1975), p. 160.
2. Ibid.

ABOVE: The beach oil fields at Goleta near Santa Barbara, bombarded by Japanese submarine, *I-17* on Feb. 23, 1942.
RIGHT: Capt. Bernard Hogen showing results of a Japanese shell hitting near the absorption plant at the Ellwood Refinery. Hogen was wounded later while trying to defuse an unexploded shell and spent 50 days in a hospital—probably the only American serviceman to receive a Purple Heart for enemy action on U.S. soil. PHOTOS COURTESY DON YOUNG, RANCHO PALOS VERDES, CALIF.

plane was reported to have crashed and burned at a Hollywood intersection and another near 185th Street and Vermont Avenue.[4]

Sergeant Everett Buckly saw no planes. Stationed in Los Angeles with the 3rd Coast Artillery, Sergeant Buckly could not "swear that there wasn't an airplane up there ... but it looked to me like a green outfit firing at its own air bursts and searchlight beam spot."[5] Bill Weller Sr.'s account of the large bright explosion is perhaps verified by Dan Tryon, who, in February 1942, was a 10-year-old magazine vendor living near Los Angeles' Mines Field.

In an attempt to impress him [Tryon], Air Corps personnel showed him a newly wrecked plane that had just been trucked into Mines Field. "This is the Jap bomber that was shot down last night," they told him. As he filled his magazine shoulder bag with souvenir parts— including a piece of blood-stained parachute harness— Tryon said, "Heck, I know a P-38 when I see one." When he went back the next day, the wrecked plane was completely gone.[6]

What did happen in the skies above Los Angeles that night? Were Japanese planes overhead? Could they have been our planes instead—commercial or private aircraft? The questions, then as now, are hotly debated. But most of what happened prior to 3:06 a.m., when the antiaircraft batteries began firing and the "air above Los Angeles erupted like a volcano," can be carefully documented. From that time on, as the official Army Air Corps history indicates, all accounts are "hopelessly at variance."[7]

Western Defense commanders in the Los Angeles area **were** jumpy the night of Feb. 24. The previous evening, while the nation listened to a Fireside Chat from President Roosevelt, the Japanese submarine *I-17* surfaced off the California coast and fired on a gaso-

3. *Los Angeles Times*, Feb. 25, 1942.
4. Ibid.
5. Webber, *Retaliation* ... , p. 160.
6. Ibid.
7. Wesley Frank Craven and James Lea Cate, *Plans and Early Operations: January 1939 to August 1940*, The Army Air Forces in World War II, Vol. 1 (Chicago: University of Chicago Press, 1948), p. 283.

104 THE WEST COAST GOES TO WAR

Left: Fire Chief C.L. Tenney of Santa Barbara in a hole from one of the 16 to 25 shells that exploded in the Goleta vicinity on Feb. 23, 1942. Top Right: Deputy Fire Chief Albert Brotherton inspects holes made in the interior of the corrugated wall of the pump house. Bottom Right: Near misses at a storage tank.
PHOTOS COURTESY DON YOUNG, RANCHO PALOS VERDES, CALIF.

line cracking plant near Santa Barbara. Negligible damage was inflicted, and the feebleness of the attack led the Western Defense Command to believe that the Santa Barbara shelling was but a diversion for the real attack that would occur farther to the south—on Los Angeles. Thus alarmed, the Army placed antiaircraft and searchlight batteries on urgent alert. Naval intelligence predicted an attack on Los Angeles within hours.

As darkness fell on the evening of Feb. 24, a number of unidentified objects in the sky over Southern California further strained the nerves of coastal defense commanders and gun crews. Flares and blinking lights were reported near aircraft plants. False alarms prompted an alert at 7:30 in the evening, but the all-clear sounded three hours later.

It would last only until the early morning hours of the next day. At 2:15 a.m., all of Los Angeles' antiaircraft batteries were put on "Green Alert" (ready to fire): Radar had detected an unidentified object 120 miles to the west, headed for the city. That was enough for the regional defense controller who ordered an immediate blackout as the object neared the coast. Abruptly, the object vanished from the radar screens, but Long Beach reported a flight of planes overhead; 25 more were reportedly seen by the coastal artillery at 12,000 feet.

An avalanche of "enemy" plane sightings now reached the Los Angeles Defense Information Station, and at 3:06 a.m. four antiaircraft batteries in Santa Monica reported seeing a balloon with a red flare. The order to commence firing was given, and the batteries roared to life.

As if on cue, every gun in the Los Angeles Basin erupted. Searchlights criss-crossed the night sky, and more than 1,400 rounds of antiaircraft shells were hurled skyward at a bizarre number of imagined targets—at phantom aircraft that dropped no bombs.

The battle ended with the dawn of the 25th. Bleary-eyed Angelinos climbed down from their rooftop vantages wondering if they had witnessed a real Japanese attack or an expensive display of fireworks. The only damage to the city came from the defenders themselves. Fragments from antiaircraft shells fell on a number of houses, and the blackout caused traffic accidents throughout the Basin, some by panicked motorists attempting to escape the "siege" by driving into the Hollywood Hills. But according to Navy Secretary Frank Knox, they could have stayed safely at home.

In Washington, Knox announced that there was no evidence of enemy planes over Los Angeles; the alert was a false alarm. The Army was not as certain, maintaining that they had spotted from one to five enemy aircraft. Secretary of War H.L. Stimson adopted the Army's version of the attack but admitted that the planes could have been civilian aircraft or enemy bombers based either in secret Mexican airfields or launched from the same submarine that fired on Santa Barbara on the 23rd.

EXTRA!

9 A.M. FINAL   Los Angeles Times   9 A.M. FINAL

VOL. LXI   WEDNESDAY MORNING, FEBRUARY 25, 1942.   DAILY, FIVE CENTS

L.A. AREA RAIDED!

Jap Planes Peril Santa Monica, Seal Beach, El Segundo, Redondo Long Beach, Hermosa, Signal Hill

Enemy Girds for Knockout Burma Blow

Reinforcements Moved Up as Defenders Fear Fall of Vital City Ne_

BY THE ASSOCIATED PRESS

Japan moved up reinforcements for the Battle of Burma and dispatched a strong naval force toward Dili, capital of Portuguese Timor, in widely separated theaters of the Pacific war today.

Australians announced a Japanese war fleet had been sighted off Dili and that invasion parachute troops had landed near Koepang, capital of the Dutch half of the island.

SHIPS REPORTED FIRED

Japanese transports in Dili Harbor, however, were reported afire and presumably this was a result of blows struck by the Dutch-Australian garrison of the Portuguese area or United Nations warplanes based on Australia or Java. The Japanese gained a foothold in both the Dutch and Portuguese sections of Timor last week.

Japanese raiders who flew at 20,000 feet killed one person and injured five yesterday in dropping 70 bombs on Port Moresby, Southern New Guinea island outpost less than 400 miles off the north tip of Australia, but were said to have caused no important damage to service buildings. The port was attacked again this afternoon.

Domei, Japanese news agency, said warships operating against Koepang had captured a Dutch freighter and a tanker.

The battle crisis heightened in

Turn to Page 2, Column 2

Today's Latest War Bulletins

BANDOENG, Feb. 25. (Æ) — Allied aircraft sank two large Japanese transport ships in a raid on a concentration near Macassar, in the Southern Celebes, and a third elsewhere, a Netherlands Indies communique said today. Allied planes also raided an aerodrome near Palembang, Japanese-occupied city in Southern Sumatra, and set three enemy planes afire, it was announced.

LONDON, Feb. 25. (Æ)—An official spokesman said today the Consul General at Batavia, capital of the Netherlands East Indies, had been arranging since last December for evacuation to Australia of British subjects in the East Indies, "particularly women and children."

TOKYO, Feb. 25. (From Japanese Broadcasts) (Æ) — Japa-

Turn to Page A, Column 6

In Colorado-- 56 Below Zero

KREMMLING (Colo.) Feb. 25. (Æ) — The temperature in this Central Colorado mountain town —not today but a week ago— was 56 degrees below zero.

The report is unofficial, from a railroad station agent's thermometer, but the weather bureau permits its publication now —for whatever aid and comfort it may give the enemy to know that Colorado can match Russian temperatures.

Fifth-Column Acts Reported During Raids

Three Japanese Seized; Mystery Movements and Lights Stir Residents

Mysterious lights, suspicious Japanese, robbery attempts marked the city's first air raid.

In the Tarzana Hills Burbank police saw a string of lights in V-form pointing toward the Lockheed aircraft plant.

Other lights were seen off Point Fermin.

Still others were reported at Redondo and in the hills back of Hermosa Beach.

Air Raid Warden Leo Schukin of Beverly Hills saw winking green and white flashes in the Windsor Hills.

Three suspicious Japanese, two men and a woman, were taken into custody on the Venice pier.

Police were called to stop prowlers who were trying to break in a bank at Laurel Canyon Drive and Ventura Blvd.

A garbage can was thrown through a jewelry store window at First and Broadway.

Home Damaged by Metal From Sky During Raid

Fragments of metal early today hailed from the sky to damage the home of Mrs. H. G. Landis, 1738 W. 43rd St., as Army searchlights and anti-aircraft fire probed the heavens for foreign planes menacing Los Angeles.

Mrs. Landis reported to author-

Turn to Page A, Column 2

Roaring out of a brilliant moonlit western sky, foreign aircraft flying both in large formation and singly, flew over Southern California early today and drew heavy barrages of anti-aircraft fire—the first ever to sound over United States continental soil against an enemy invader.

No bombs were reported dropped.

At 5 a.m. the police reported that an airplane had been shot down near 185th St. and Vermont Ave. Details were not available. Earlier, the Fourth Air Force in San Francisco said that at least one plane had been downed in the raid.

Sirens shrieked throughout the Southland at 2:23 a.m., and an immediate blackout was enforced.

Almost instantly the great fingers of light from the giant Army searchlights shot into the sky, clustering first in an area appearing above the vast El Segundo oil refineries.

Simultaneously the anti-aircraft defenses of the city roared into action and soon the entire southwestern skies of the city were ablaze with orange bursts.

The planes, flying in number variously estimated at from 8 to 20, flew at an altitude of

Turn to Page A, Column 1

Newspaper headlines exploded across Los Angeles on Feb. 25, 1942, with erroneous reports that enemy planes had raided Southern California. It was also reported that there were fifth-column (sabotage) acts in the area. This was all in error as no United States city was ever attacked by enemy planes nor was any sabotage carried out by Japanese living in this country. The west coast was in a constant state of alert until the great naval victory at Midway in early June 1942. After the battle the potential threat by the Japanese was greatly diminished.

In Southern California, hardly anyone was satisfied with any official explanation. If the attack was real, why were no Army Air Corps interceptor planes sent out against the enemy aircraft? And if the planes were civilian, where did they go after flying over Los Angeles?

Stimson had no answers, but the *Los Angeles Times* had questions. An editorial on the 26th deplored the alert's wreaking "considerable public excitement and confusion" but warned that the "spectacular official accompaniments," in the form of Knox and Stimson's explanations, were unacceptable to the West Coast.

Who Flew? The controversy of the battle of Los Angeles will no doubt continue as long as witnesses are alive to recall it. Probably no one flew. If the phantom aircraft were enemy bombers or reconnaissance planes, where did they come from? The nearest Japanese aircraft carrier was thousands of miles away in the Northern Pacific. The Japanese submarine that shelled the Santa Barbara coast on the 23rd was equipped with a small, two-seater reconnaissance plane. But her commander stated in 1945 that he had launched no aircraft that night—certainly not so puny an airplane as his. And the existence of Secretary Stimson's mysterious Mexican airfields strains our credibility now as much as it did in 1942.

Perhaps the best explanation was provided by Wendell Willkie, who had experienced the real thing in the London blitz. Willkie, the Republican nominee for president in 1940, told the West Coast that when a real air raid occurred, "you won't have to argue about it—you'll just know."[8]

FOR THE WEST COAST, the Battle of Los Angeles and the shellings at Santa Barbara sharply punctuated the succession of bad news from the fronts and especially reinforced the collective fear that the enemy could attack virtually at will and virtually wherever on the coast he wanted. Publicly, General DeWitt assured the Pacific Coast that defenses were adequate and could repel any aerial attack. Privately—and urgently—he pleaded with Washington to send more bombers, pursuit planes, and antiaircraft guns and crews. The Western Defense Command estimated (in private memos) that the shipyards and aircraft plants even in the largest and best-defended cities could not sustain a concerted attack. Defenses were too thin and the crews manning the guns too green.

In the Pacific, the news got worse. In March, a combined fleet of Dutch and American warships failed to halt the Japanese conquest of the Dutch East Indies. The engagement was called the Battle of the Java Sea, and the Allied squadron was soundly defeated by the Japanese navy. The U.S. heavy cruiser *Houston* was sunk with a loss of 1,000 lives.

Then, at last, some better news: General Douglas MacArthur had escaped from the Philippines. Realizing the fate of the beleaguered American and Filipino armies, Roosevelt ordered his popular commander to leave Bataan and direct the Pacific war from Australia. In the midst of so troubling a time, a nation desperately needing a lift to its spirits, however small, made MacArthur a hero overnight. He was celebrated in song ("Fightin' Doug MacArthur") and in civic pride on the West Coast. Los Angeles renamed Westlake Park after him, and farther to the south in Orange County, MacArthur Boulevard appeared in Santa Ana. But all that could not help Bataan, which fell on April 9. And spirits on the West Coast fell with it, only to be lifted a few weeks later.

On April 19, banner headlines in West Coast newspapers announced the electrifying news that Tokyo had been bombed. Taking off from a secret air base—President Roosevelt mysteriously called it "Shangri-La"—16 B-25 Mitchell bombers under the command of Gen. James Doolittle had attacked the Japanese mainland.[9] The damage inflicted was minimal, but the **fact** of the raid itself—the fact that Japan was vulnerable—was a tonic for the nation and came at a time when it was sorely needed. Assembly-line workers at the North American Aviation plant in Los Angeles, where the Mitchell bombers had been built, stopped work and cheered at the news.

The Doolittle Raid was a success. But it was not to be had without consequences, and the consequences for the West Coast appeared serious indeed. Japanese radio messages, intercepted and decoded by navy intelligence, indicated that retaliation against the West Coast might be imminent. "The Japanese," Stimson confided to General Marshall, "have lost face by this attack on them ... and ... will counterattack on us with carriers." And the logical and most vulnerable place to attack was the American Pacific Coast.

From April and well into May, West Coast air defenses were strengthened, and the War Department advised General DeWitt to prepare for the attack likely to come after May 10. Now the teletype lines between Washington and the Presidio fairly crackled with warning messages arriving almost daily. Marshall warned DeWitt to expect "hit-and-run raids on West Coast cities of the

---

8. Cited in the *Los Angeles Times*, Feb. 28, 1942.
9. Actually, the B-25s took off from the aircraft carrier *Hornet*, 600 miles from the Japanese mainland.

Top: B-25s crowd the *Hornet*'s flight deck. The carrier could accommodate only 16 bombers if there was to be enough room to take off. USN NH53426 Bottom: A B-25 takes off for its historic mission over Japan. USAF

VOL. CLXXVI, NO. 108   CCCC* *   SAN FRANCISCO, SATURDAY, APRIL 18, 1942   DAILY, 5 CENTS, SUNDAY, 12 CENTS DAILY AND SUNDAY PER MONTH $1.40*

U. S. BOMBERS BLAST TOKIO AND YOKOHAMA

IN THE NEWS

Saturday Symposium
Los Angeles, Calif.
April 15, 1942.
Mr. William Randolph Hearst
Los Angeles Examiner
Los Angeles, Calif.

Dear Mr. Hearst:

THE increasing importance of women in this war is going to result in a more economic democracy for women of America, when the war is over, than has ever been known before in the history of America.

The need for American women and their willingness and ability to learn in this conflict is breaking down all sorts of barriers that have handicapped us before.

It is daily proving that they have the resources, energy, and determination that can be of benefit to the Nation when at war as well as peace.

The American women who braved the wilderness of the New World, the women who went west in the covered wagons, and all the other incomparable women of our country have shown their ability and determination in the building and preservation of this wonderful country of ours.

Today the American woman is doing her job—in the field and factory, in the home and hospital, in club, clinic and her community. She is learning that some war work is dull and drab; that some is dangerous and dramatic, but all of it is very important to America.

She is serving everywhere and any place she is needed from volunteer services to working in airplane factories, and in a great many instances in the aircraft factories she proves more satisfactory than men.

The American women are carrying their full share of the war in the factories, in public service, and in the full support of our army at the front.

American women will learn much from this war that will benefit them to take their place in the world after war.

In my travels throughout the Nation from one coast to another, I talk with the American women and discuss the various problems and it is very self evident the trend is towards a new economic picture for our women.

One young lady I talked with in an eastern plant where she was healing out sheet iron, said the first few days she tired a little from her work, but after that she went right on, and she enjoyed her work more and more every day.

Our women are serving or working in all phases of defense and are holding high the morale of the American women, thereby paving the way for a new economic deal.

(Continued on Page A, Col. 4)

Japs Admit Fires, Damage; 9 Planes Reported Downed

TOKIO, (From Japanese Broadcasts), April 18 (Saturday)—(AP)—Allied battle planes — identified here as American — swooped upon the Tokio-Yokohama region with fire and explosive bombs for the first time today and fear of their lethal cargoes prompted air raid warnings across more than 800 miles of the Japanese archipelago.

Japanese observers declared the red, white and blue star ensign could be seen plainly on the planes.

The long reaches of Honshu, Japan's major island; Shikoku, which nestles in the lower arm of Honshu, and Hokkaido, to the north were under alerts or the bombsights of the raiders for hours, Japanese announcements disclosed.

Fires, casualties and damage were left in the wake of the squadrons, from which it was authoritatively announced that nine planes were shot down.

Broadcasts in Japanese, Chinese and English reported the details.

A Chinese language announcement said the raiders flew "American airplanes." (This might mean that the crews were from the United States. However, American built craft have been assigned to British, Dutch, Australian and Chinese forces, as well as to Soviet Russia, technically a neutral in the Pacific war.)

"The imperial family is safe," a communique said.

Central defense headquarters announced that two enemy planes had raided Nagoya, a manufacturing center 170 miles southwest of Tokio, and that a single aircraft spilled incendiaries over the port of Kobe, another 100 miles southwest. The announcement said "no serious damage was caused."

"The enemy planes approached Tokio from several directions," said a communique of Emperor Hirohito's Imperial headquarters.

In San Francisco last night, just before the Japanese official announcement was made, the CBS lis-

(Continued on Page 3, Col. 3)

U. S. BOMBERS AGAIN BLAST RANGOON DOCKS

NEW DELHI, April 18 (Saturday)—(AP)—A squadron of United States heavy bombers raided Japanese occupied Rangoon in Burma Thursday, it was announced officially today.

The text of the communique follows:

"A squadron of our heavy bombers made a raid on Rangoon on the night of April 16. "Docks and harbor installations were heavily bombed. "Although intense antiaircraft fire was encountered, no damage was sustained either by our bombers or personnel."

By The Associated Press.
NEW DELHI (India), April 17.—British sappers burned and blasted 6,000 West Burma oil wells today while a gallant battalion of the King's own Yorkshire Light Infantry fought yet another superb delaying action against the Japanese until the wells were ablaze.

Then the vastly outnumbered Yorkshiremen withdrew and rejoined the main British Imperial forces after inflicting severe casualties.

A communique placed the positions "north of Magwe," indicating the troops were even now amid the ruined wells. Magwe is on the southern gateway to the field centering around Yenangyaung, twenty miles north.

CITED FOR GALLANTRY.
The British communique cited the Yorkshire force "distinguished itself in this gallant action with great determination and bravery and suffered very little loss."

It was the sort of action that has won this handful of men two

(Continued on Page 3, Col. 4)

Laval Meets Snag; Leahy Called Home

U. S. Acts in First Show Of Teeth

By MICHAEL CHINIGO
Staff Correspondent Int'l News Service
WASHINGTON, April 17.—President Roosevelt, in an initial show of teeth against Vichy's capitulation to Adolf Hitler, today summarily recalled Ambassador William D. Leahy from his French post "for consultation."

The President's move was announced by Acting Secretary of State Welles even as Pierre Laval labored in Vichy to maneuver Marshal Petain and Admiral Darlan into subordination to himself and his pro-Nazi collaborationist cabinet.

TO STEEL RESISTANCE.
Leahy's recall was directed toward steeling the resistance of French leaders and the French people against the Nazi-inspired coup and disavowing beforehand, Laval's expected bid for continued United States French amity. America's action, Welles explained,

(Continued on Page A, Col. 2)

Mrs. H. P. Whitney Dies in New York

NEW YORK, April 18.—(AP)—Mrs. Harry Payne Whitney, 67, widow of the financier, died at 5:30 a. m. today in New York hospital from heart complications.

Dentz Named As Scorning Nazi Post

VICHY, April 17.—(AP)—After three days of continuous conversations among the leaders of the old and new regimes, pro-German Pierre Laval was still understood to be lacking two names for his government to replace the cabinet which today handed its resignation to Marshal Petain.

The discussions which Laval has been carrying on with politicians and technicians resembled the ministerial crises of pre-war days and brought about combinations of party groups, some of which have been suppressed by Vichy.

The difficulties encountered were shown by the fact that it was first announced the Cabinet would be made known Thursday. It was then put off until noon today and finally postponed until tomorrow.

REFUSE TO SERVE.
Reliable foreign diplomatic sources said Laval was encountering difficulty in persuading some of his choices as Cabinet ministers to take jobs in the collaborationist government.

The names of the candidates who objected to taking positions in the government are not known but it was rumored that Gen. Henri Dentz, former commander in chief of the French forces in the Levant and high commissioner to Syria, was rumored to be one of those who held back acceptance.

Petain took no part in the deliberations with Cabinet prospects, merely observing and awaiting the list.

BERLIN FORECAST.
(From Bern, the course of France's new leaders was forecast thus:

(LAVAL: He will, as head of the Government, seek to achieve internal calm while carrying on negotiations with Germany which may bring a break with the United States.

(DARLAN: In control of the Government, will have the final say if France is brought to the point of battle again, as the result either of an

600 British Planes Raid Germany

Day-Long Raids on Reich; Hamburg Bombed

By DREW MIDDLETON
Associated Press Staff Writer.
LONDON, April 18 (Saturday).—The Royal Air Force hammered enemy territory again during the night after hurling 600 planes against German targets in day long raids extending from the continental coast to Augsburg, in southern Germany.

(Berlin reported an attack on Hamburg with five enemy planes shot down.)

In small scale retaliation, the German air force bombed a few places in southern England early today and the Government said "damage caused was not excessive but there were some casualties, including a small number of persons killed."

One German aircraft was destroyed during the night over England.

British air superiority over western Europe was stressed by

(Continued on Page 5, Col. 3)

Russ Planes Blast Nazis in Norway

LONDON, April 18 (Saturday)—(UNS)—Wave after wave of Red Army bombers raided Nazi troop concentrations at Vardo, Norway, the Daily Telegraph reported today.

At least seventy Soviet bombers carried out the raids, concentrating on German barracks and killing more than 200 Germans, according to the report, quoting the Norwegian telegraph agency.

The barracks were believed to have housed at least 2,000 Nazi troops. Vardo is on the extreme eastern tip of Norway on the Arctic Ocean.

lack of the day before when more than 400 planes were used.

Emphasizing the scope of the aerial offensive was a daylight attack upon Ausburg, which involved a roundtrip of at least 1,000 miles right over the heart of industrial Germany.

Augsburg, a few miles northwest of Munich, is the site of a Messerschmitt plane factory, but an informed source said this extablishment was not the target of today's raiders. This center was the target of night raids twice in August, 1940, but had not been mentioned in British air communiques since then.

British air superiority over western Europe was stressed by

(Continued on Page 5, Col. 3)

Corregidor Smashes Jap Siege Batteries

WASHINGTON, April 17.—(AP)—The guns of the Manila Bay forts silenced three Japanese artillery batteries in the past twenty-four hours, the War Department reported today, adding that an enemy bomber was hit and was believed to have crashed.

A late day communique said that on the Island of Panay, about 150 miles south of the Philippine forts, fierce fighting was believed to be in progress between defending troops and an enemy invasion force which effected landings at the Cities of Iloilo and Capiz.

Corregidor and nearby Caballo Island, the site of Fort Hughes, were raided five times by enemy bombers, flying in formations of from two to eight planes each, the Department said.

The text of the communique, based on reports received here up to 8 p. m. (2 p. m. S. F. time):

"1—Philippine theater:

"Three enemy batteries, firing on our forts from Cavite and Bataan, were silenced by our artillery fire during the past twenty-four hours.

"Corregidor and Caballo Islands were raided five times by enemy bombers, flying in formations of from two to eight planes. One Japanese bomber was hit by our antiaircraft fire and damaged to such an extent that it is believed to have crashed, though its destruction was not confirmed.

"Fierce fighting is reported from Papay, where the enemy landed at Iloilo and Capiz.

(Continued on Page 3, Col. 4)

Russ Battering at Gateway to Smolensk, Threaten Encirclement

LONDON, April 17.—(AP)—Stockholm dispatches said raiding columns in White Russia, west of the city, were handicapping German efforts to rush up reinforcements.

This agreed with the Russian report of assaults around Demidov, strengthening an impression that the Russians might be starting an encirclement maneuver.

Heavy fighting also was reported between Lakes Ilmen, Ladoga and Onega, as the Russians sought to erase the menace to Leningrad before the thaws convert roads into bogs and streams into torrents.

Russian and other accounts indicated the fighting north of Lake men was possibly the heaviest in recent weeks.

Belief that large Soviet forces were employed in the assaults was based partly on a German announcement earlier this week that the German Air Force was attacking Russian troops and tank concentrations along the crossings which remained usable.

Still farther north, between Lakes Ladoga and Onega, the Finns acknowledged that the Finns were hammering at their lines in a major offensive now six days old. The Finns claimed they were holding firm, however, and that Russian attempts to storm their positions were costly failures.

Apartment Hunters! See Details Examiner Free Rental Service, Page 24

continental United States supported by heavy naval forces."

More barrage balloons were added to Seattle, and sandboxes for extinguishing incendiary bombs appeared on street corners. General DeWitt's earlier pleas for additional planes and antiaircraft batteries were finally answered, as the army sent two bomber groups and more coastal defense units. Marshall himself inspected the West Coast defenses and was appalled, recommending further reinforcements for San Diego and Los Angeles. Never had the Pacific Coast, civilian and military alike, been more alarmed and apprehensive.

Then, on the 16th, came the poison gas scare. After the capitulation of Guam, the Japanese announced the discovery of poison gas on the island. Claiming the United States had "abrogated the poison-gas clause of international law," the Japanese warned that "Uncle Sam's boys will be given a smell of their own DuPont gas which the Japanese captured at Guam."

That announcement, and the fact that the U.S. Navy had discovered *Japanese* gas on a captured ship, threw the West Coast into further panic. DeWitt was warned to expect a gas attack at any time, and he received 350,000 gas masks and decontamination equipment from Washington. Practice alerts and drills were staged in San Francisco. In the event of an attack civilians were advised to close all doors and windows and head for the roof. In Los Angeles, the warnings were a bit more puckish. "Immediately before entering a house," the city health officials warned, "remove your outer clothing. Don't hesitate to do this. It's better to have a red face than a burned body." The Army Chemical Corps designed a gas mask with a Mickey Mouse face for children.[10]

So great now was the apprehension, the Western Defense Command was placed on special alert. Full-strength regimental combat teams supplemented coastal defense units, and the War Department advised General DeWitt that "surprise attacks on the West Coast are a possibility from now on." And the West Coast waited.

But the attacks never came. The enemy, wisely or not, had other, safer, and less ambitious plans. The Japanese Imperial Command and, indeed, the Japanese civilian population had been shocked by the Doolittle Raid. The American B-25s inflicted only token damage, but the raid itself profoundly impressed Japanese military strategists. If a small American naval force could penetrate Japan's defenses so easily, could steam within 600 sea miles of the home islands and launch warplanes, then so perhaps could a larger force, one comprising heavier bombers. And they could be based not on aircraft carriers, but at island airfields near Japan. Clearly, the home islands were vulnerable.

Accordingly, after the Doolittle Raid, Japanese military planning turned defensive. The territory won since Pearl Harbor was to be protected. The offensive would be continued only in strategically vital areas, such as Southeast Asia, which contained the raw materials of the Imperial engines of war—rubber, metals, foodstuffs and oil.

To the Imperial navy fell the task of defense: the consolidation of a rim of naval steel in the Pacific, from the Aleutians in the north, bulging slightly at the Marshall and Gilbert islands in the middle, and anchored in the south at the Coral Sea off Australia. But to secure the middle, Japan needed Midway Island.

Thus on May 20, 1942, two large task forces of the Imperial navy cleared their ports in Japan and Saipan and steamed for the Central Pacific. By now their intentions were clear. United States naval intelligence, having broken the Japanese "Purple" and "Magic" codes, knew that Midway was the target. The U.S. task force under Admiral Nimitz steamed out of San Diego and Pearl Harbor to meet them.

The Japanese were soundly beaten. Unable to sustain the loss of four aircraft carriers, Admiral Yamamoto's forces retired. And the Battle of Midway, easily the most important naval engagement of the Pacific war, at last restored the balance of naval power. Never again could the Japanese fleet threaten the West Coast. To do so they would have to fight another Midway.

So the West Coast breathed easier. Three days after Midway, General DeWitt ended the special alert. West Coast antiaircraft gunners and pursuit planes stood down. No more blackouts, dimouts, or alerts. No more panic. No more hysteria.

The Battle of Midway conveniently marks the end of our story. But for the West Coast, and the rest of the nation, those crucial days in early June 1942 were only the end of the beginning. The war went on, its greatest dramas yet to be played. Fortunately for the Pacific Coast, the drama to follow would not unfold on the beaches of California, Oregon and Washington.

The months after Pearl Harbor would bring food and gasoline rationing, "Meatless Tuesdays," D-Day, and the atomic bomb. The months would also continue the disruption and utter change wrought by Pearl

---

10. But no child on the West Coast ever wore one. Making the Mickey Mouse ears required too much rubber, and the project was dropped.

Harbor and the West Coast's participation in a global conflict of unprecedented size and scope.

Utter change indeed. That the Second World War changed the United States is a truism that need scarcely to be explored in these pages. A war of such global proportions affected Americans like no other conflict ever had—or perhaps ever would. It was a war that, literally, touched everyone: from servicemen and Gold Star mothers to defense workers; from school children practicing for air raids to the yet-unborn of the post-war baby boom. None were exempt. And when it was all over, no one would ever be the same.

Nowhere was that change so acute and so noticeable as it was on America's West Coast. Washington, Oregon, and California were vulnerable—especially in the war's first six months—to the tide of battle that raged in the Pacific. Every defeat, every victory, every rumor, every threat of attack, however real, rippled across the Pacific Ocean and sent shock waves that eventually broke on our shore. We were closer to the enemy. He had struck the first blow uncomfortably near. And from Pearl Harbor to Midway, the West Coast was never quite disabused of the possibility that he would strike even closer.

The *USS Hornet* (CV-8) was commissioned in late 1941. The carrier carried the 16 B-25s to bomb Japan in April 1942. She was sunk in the Battle of Santa Cruz in October 1942. USN NH81313

Aerial view of the two strategic islands that make up the Midway Atoll, San Island in the background, Eastern Island in the foreground. NA 80-G-451086

CHAPTER EIGHT

Photo Potpourri

Top: Sign on top of a union hall in Seattle, Wash., March 1942. Bottom: Sign at Yakima, Wash., September 1941. LC

ABOVE LEFT: Standing at ease are members of the Roosevelt High School, Los Angeles, Victory Corps Girls. Riflery was one of many war-related activities offered at the school. FDR LIBRARY ABOVE RIGHT: Larrie Lou Osterman sits on her front steps in McMinnville, Ore., with her toys; which will go to the scrap drive.

RIGHT: Jimmy Hargis won $150 in 1942 for the most scrap metal collected in Oregon. He then started collecting for the paper drive.

These men were organized as the Lincoln County Guerillas in Oregon. They were training to repel a possible Japanese invasion, April 1942.

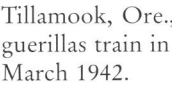

Aircraft Warning Service observers in Gresham, Ore., receive armbands for identification.

Tillamook, Ore., guerillas train in March 1942.

**Headquarters
Western Defense Command
and Fourth Army**

Presidio of San Francisco, California

- - -

Public Proclamation No. 3

- - -

March 24, 1942

TO: The people within the States of Washington, Oregon, California, Montana, Idaho, Nevada, Utah and Arizona, and the Public Generally:

WHEREAS, By Public Proclamation No. 1, dated March 2, 1942, this headquarters, there were designated and established Military Areas Nos. 1 and 2 and Zones thereof, and

WHEREAS, By Public Proclamation No. 2, dated March 16, 1942, this headquarters, there were designated and established Military Areas Nos. 3, 4, 5 and 6 and Zones thereof, and

WHEREAS, The present situation within these Military Areas and Zones requires as a matter of military necessity the establishment of certain regulations pertaining to all enemy aliens and all persons of Japanese ancestry within said Military Areas and Zones thereof:

Now, THEREFORE, I, J. L. DEWITT, Lieutenant General, U. S. Army, by virtue of the authority vested in me by the President of the United States and by the Secretary of War and my powers and prerogatives as Commanding General, Western Defense Command, do hereby declare and establish the following regulations covering the conduct to be observed by all alien Japanese, all alien Germans, all alien Italians, and all persons of Japanese ancestry residing or being within the Military Areas above described, or such portions thereof as are hereinafter mentioned:

1. From and after 6:00 A. M., March 27, 1942, all alien Japanese, all alien Germans, all alien Italians, and all persons of Japanese ancestry residing or being within the geographical limits of Military Area No. 1, or within any of the Zones established within Military Area No. 2, as those areas are defined and described in Public Proclamation No. 1, dated March 2, 1942, this headquarters, or within the geographical limits of the designated Zones established within Military Areas Nos. 3, 4, 5, and 6, as those areas are defined and described in Public Proclamation No. 2, dated March 16, 1942, this headquarters, or within any of such additional Zones as may hereafter be similarly designated and defined, shall be within their place of residence between the hours of 8:00 P. M. and 6:00 A. M., which period is hereinafter referred to as the hours of curfew.

2. At all other times all such persons shall be only at their place of residence or employment or traveling between those places or within a distance of not more than five miles from their place of residence.

3. Nothing in paragraph 2 shall be construed to prohibit any of the above specified persons from visiting the nearest United States Post Office, United States Employment Service Office, or office operated or maintained by the Wartime Civil Control Administration, for the purpose of transacting any business or the making of any arrangements reasonably necessary to accomplish evacuation; nor be construed to prohibit travel under duly issued change of residence notice and travel permit provided for in paragraph 5 of Public Proclamations Numbers 1 and 2. Travel performed in change of residence to a place outside the prohibited and restricted areas may be performed without regard to curfew hours.

4. Any person violating these regulations will be subject to immediate exclusion from the Military Areas and Zones specified in paragraph 1 and to the criminal penalties provided by Public Law No. 503, 77th Congress, approved March 21, 1942, entitled: "An Act to Provide a Penalty for Violation of Restrictions or Orders with Respect to Persons Entering, Remaining in, Leaving or Committing Any Act in Military Areas or Zone." In the case of any alien enemy, such person will in addition be subject to immediate apprehension and internment.

5. By subsequent proclamation or order there will be prescribed those classes of persons who will be entitled to apply for exemptions from exclusion orders hereafter to be issued. Persons granted such exemption will likewise and at the same time also be exempted from the operation of the curfew regulations of this proclamation.

6. After March 31, 1942, no person of Japanese ancestry shall have in his possession or use or operate at any time or place within any of the Military Areas 1 to 6 inclusive, as established and defined in Public Proclamations Nos. 1 and 2, above mentioned any of the following items:
   (a) Firearms.
   (b) Weapons or implements of war or component parts thereof.
   (c) Ammunition.
   (d) Bombs.
   (e) Explosives or the component parts thereof.
   (f) Short-wave radio receiving sets having a frequency of 1,750 kilocycles or greater or of 540 kilocycles or less.
   (g) Radio transmitting sets.
   (h) Signal devices.
   (i) Codes or ciphers.
   (j) Cameras.

Any such person found in possession of any of the above named items in violation of the foregoing will be subject to the criminal penalties provided by Public Law No. 503, 77th Congress, approved March 21, 1942, entitled: "An Act to Provide a Penalty for Violation of Restrictions or Orders with Respect to Persons Entering, Remaining in, Leaving or Committing Any Act in Military Areas or Zone."

7. The regulations herein prescribed with reference to the observance of curfew hours by enemy aliens, are substituted for and supersede the regulations of the United States Attorney General heretofore in force in certain limited areas. All curfew exemptions heretofore granted by the United States Attorneys are hereby revoked effective as of 6:00 a. m., PWT, March 27, 1942.

8. The Federal Bureau of Investigation is designated as the agency to enforce the foregoing provisions. It is requested that the civil police within the states affected by this Proclamation assist the Federal Bureau of Investigation by reporting to it the names and addresses of all persons believed to have violated these regulations.

J. L. DEWITT
Lieutenant General, U. S. Army
Commanding

HEADQUARTERS WESTERN DEFENSE COMMAND AND FOURTH ARMY

Presidio of San Francisco, California

Public Proclamation No. 4

March 27, 1942

TO: The people within the States of Washington, Oregon, California, Montana, Idaho, Nevada, Utah and Arizona, and the Public Generally:

WHEREAS, By Public Proclamation No. 1, dated March 2, 1942, this headquarters, there was designated and established Military Area No. 1, and

WHEREAS, It is necessary, in order to provide for the welfare and to insure the orderly evacuation and resettlement of Japanese voluntarily migrating from Military Area No. 1, to restrict and regulate such migration:

NOW, THEREFORE, I, J. L. DEWITT, Lieutenant General, U. S. Army, by virtue of the authority vested in me by the President of the United States and by the Secretary of War and my powers and prerogatives as Commanding General, Western Defense Command, do hereby declare that the present situation requires as a matter of military necessity that, commencing at 12:00 midnight, P. W. T., March 29, 1942, all alien Japanese and persons of Japanese ancestry who are within the limits of Military Area No. 1, be and they are hereby prohibited from leaving that area for any purpose until and to the extent that a future proclamation or order of this headquarters shall so permit or direct.

Any person violating this proclamation will be subject to the criminal penalties provided by Public Law No. 503, 77th Congress, approved March 21, 1942, entitled: "An Act to Provide a Penalty for Violation of Restrictions or Orders with Respect to Persons Entering, Remaining in, Leaving or Committing Any Act in Military Areas or Zones." In the case of any alien enemy, such person will in addition be subject to immediate apprehension and internment.

J. L. DEWITT
Lieutenant General, U. S. Army
Commanding

**Headquarters
Western Defense Command
and Fourth Army**

Presidio of San Francisco, California

Public Proclamation
No. 5

March 30, 1942

TO: The people within the States of Washington, Oregon, California, Montana, Idaho, Nevada, Utah and Arizona, and the Public Generally:

WHEREAS, by Public Proclamation No. 1, dated March 2, 1942, this headquarters, there were designated and established Military Areas Nos. 1 and 2 and Zones thereof, and

WHEREAS, by Public Proclamation No. 2, dated March 16, 1942, this headquarters, there were designated and established Military Areas Nos. 3, 4, 5 and 6 and Zones thereof, and

WHEREAS, the present situation within these Military Areas and Zones requires as a matter of military necessity the establishment of certain regulations, as set forth hereinafter:

NOW, THEREFORE, I, J. L. DEWITT, Lieutenant General, U. S. Army, by virtue of the authority vested in me by the President of the United States and by the Secretary of War and my powers and prerogatives as Commanding General, Western Defense Command, do hereby declare and establish the following regulations covering the conduct to be observed by all alien Japanese, all alien Germans, all alien Italians, and all persons of Japanese ancestry residing or being within the Military Areas above described:

Prior to and during the period of exclusion and evacuation of certain persons or classes of persons from prescribed Military Areas and Zones, persons otherwise subject thereto but who come within one or more of the classes specified in (a), (b), (c), (d), (e) and (f), following, may make written application for exemption from such exclusion and evacuation. Application Form WDC-PM 5 has been prepared for that purpose and copies thereof may be procured from any United States Post Office or United States Employment Service office in the Western Defense Command by persons who deem themselves entitled to exemption.

The following classes of persons are hereby authorized to be exempted from exclusion and evacuation upon the furnishing of satisfactory proof as specified in Form WDC-PM 5:

(a) German and Italian aliens seventy or more years of age.

(b) In the case of German and Italian aliens, the parent, wife, husband, child of (or other person who resides in the household and whose support is wholly dependent upon) an officer, enlisted man or commissioned nurse on active duty in the Army of the United States (or any component thereof), U. S. Navy, U. S. Marine Corps, or U. S. Coast Guard.

(c) In the case of German and Italian aliens, the parent, wife, husband, child of (or other person who resides in the household and whose support is wholly dependent upon) an officer, enlisted man or commissioned nurse who on or since December 7, 1941, died in line of duty with the armed services of the United States indicated in the preceding subparagraph.

(d) German and Italian aliens awaiting naturalization who had filed a petition for naturalization and who had paid the filing fee therefor in a court of competent jurisdiction on or before December 7, 1941.

(e) Patients in hospital, or confined elsewhere, and too ill or incapacitated to be removed therefrom without danger to life.

(f) Inmates of orphanages and the totally deaf, dumb or blind.

The applicant for exemption will be required to furnish the kinds of proof specified in Form WDC-PM 5 in support of the application. The certificate of exemption from evacuation will also include exemption from compliance with curfew regulations, subject, however, to such future proclamations or orders in the premises as may from time to time be issued by this headquarters. The person to whom such exemption from evacuation and curfew has been granted shall thereafter be entitled to reside in any portion of any prohibited area, including those areas heretofore declared prohibited by the Attorney General of the United States.

J. L. DEWITT
*Lieutenant General, U. S. Army
Commanding*

Naval reservists from the San Francisco Bay area report on board the USS *Delta Queen* (YHB-7), after being called to active duty in 1940. The *Delta Queen* served as a Navy barracks and training ship at Yerba Buena and Treasure islands in San Francisco Bay, between 1940 and 1946.

"Jinx to the Japs" sponsored by the El Cerrito, Calif., Chamber of Commerce, Feb. 13, 1942.

Red Cross volunteers wrapped bandages at the San Francisco headquarters, Dec. 8, 1941. LC

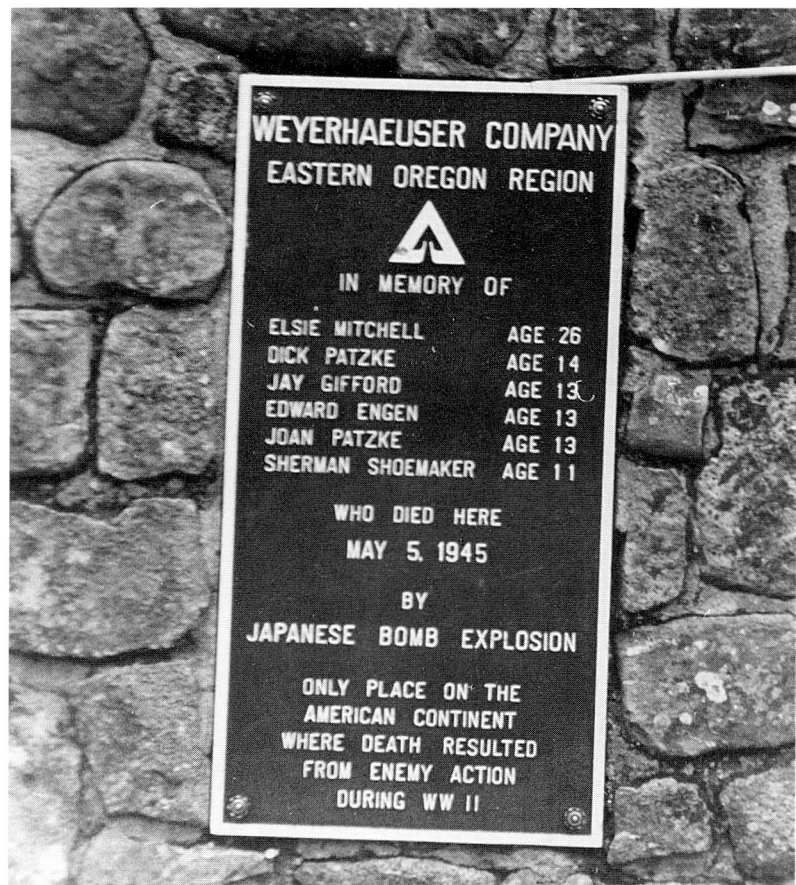

ABOVE: A lone sentinel walks his post at Ft. Funston as twilight silhouettes him against the Pacific. San Francisco, Calif., 25 November 1942. By September 1945 the lights were back on, not only on the West Coast but all over America.

RIGHT: Monument plaque at the site of the Japanese balloon bomb explosion.

CHAPTER NINE

Legacy of the War

WWII'S SUNKEN TANKERS RAISE SPILL THREAT

by David Kligman
Associated Press

SAN FRANCISCO—On the Pacific Ocean floor just a mile outside the nation's largest marine sanctuary lies the *Montebello*, a World War II-era tanker filled with more than 3 million gallons of crude oil.

The discovery last month has experts debating what to do with the tanker, which was torpedoed by the Japanese 16 days after the bombing of Pearl Harbor in 1941.

Do authorities do nothing and wait until the tanker eventually corrodes, possibly leaking globs of oil into the Monterey Bay National Marine Sanctuary? Do they try pumping the oil from the 440-foot tanker?

And shouldn't this raise concerns along the East Coast and Gulf of Mexico, where German U-boats wreaked havoc early in WWII?

The Atlantic Foundation, a Wilmington, N.C.-based environmental research group, warns that hundreds of tankers and freighters are submerged along the eastern seaboard and contain untold millions of gallons of fuel and toxic materials.

"We've really swept a lot of things under the rug," said Mike Jordan, the group's director. "How much are we gambling by not really knowing what's out there?"

Though last month's discovery off Cambria, Calif., appeared dire, maritime archaeologist Jack Hunter said there is no immediate threat of a major oil leak from the tanker, which lies in 900 feet of water just south of the 5,000-square mile marine sanctuary.

The 46-degree water has hardened the *Montebello*'s 3.1 million gallons of oil into a substance with the consistency somewhere between tar and Jell-O. Barring a catastrophic earthquake, Hunter said it's a safe bet it will be years before the tanker breaks apart.

Hunter recommends the ship be monitored over the next 10 years until technology is developed to draw oil out of the tanker without the danger of a spill.

"At some point we're going to have to deal with this," said Hunter, who led last month's expedition to the Montebello's final resting place.

Ronald Tjeerdema, a University of California-Santa Cruz chemistry professor, questioned whether extreme measures are needed.

In the case of the *Montebello*, Tjeerdema said one solution might be to punch a hole in the ship to let the oil slowly seep for the next 10 years. He said his suggestion, while not politically correct, would disperse the oil without overwhelming the environment.

"It probably wouldn't be very popular, but it would be a way of ameliorating the threat of a major spill," Tjeerdema said. "Most people don't realize that when oil is spilled, most of it is degraded by natural processes. By letting it seep at a very slow rate we're actually letting nature take care of it."

Rose Pfund, who studies oil spills, said it would be a waste of money to try to pump oil from sunken tankers. Barring a major catastrophe, the environment can handle it, she said.

"The USS *Arizona* to this day releases oil into Pearl Harbor ever since it was sunk in 1941," said Pfund, associate director of the Sea Grant College Program in Honolulu.

Above: The aftermath of V-J Day on Market Street in San Francisco, with the Ferry Building in the far background, a street car heads up Market Street as sailors and civilians still parade up and down the sidewalks. This view is at California Street and Grant Avenue. Facing page: This famous Gabrial Moulin photograph was also taken on Market Street on V-J Day. MOULIN STUDIOS

Fort MacArthur Museum at Angels Gate Park, San Pedro, Calif.

Fort MacArthur Museum

IN 1985 the Fort MacArthur Museum was established in the corridors and galleries of historic Battery Osgood-Farley. Battery Osgood-Farley is the only unmodified of its type and vintage in the continental United States and may well be the best preserved example of a U.S. Army seacoast gun battery. The museum is dedicated to the preservation and interpretation of the history of Fort MacArthur, a U.S. Army post which guarded the Los Angeles harbor from 1914 to 1974.

The Fort MacArthur Reservations hold an important collection of historical structures tied to the U.S. Army's role in the defense of the American continental coastline from invasion. These structures, which are interpreted at the museum, clearly trace the development of American coastal defenses, from the all-gun era of the turn of the century to missile era of today.

The museum is administered by the City of Los Angeles Department of Recreation & Parks and is located at Angels Gate Park in San Pedro, Calif.

DECEMBER 9, 1941.—[PART I.]

Ft. MacArthur Area Ordered Evacuated

Evacuation of some 200 women and children—the families of Army officers—from the Ft. MacArthur military reservation was virtually complete early last night.

Col. William W. Hicks, commandant of the Harbor Defense Area, ordered the evacuation as a safety measure at 4 p.m. yesterday.

The families left their quarters provided by the government and scattered to furnished homes and apartments in the harbor area and near-by cities, it was reported.

At the same time, Col. Hicks advised Sheriff Eugene W. Biscailuz, as chairman of the Los Angeles County Defense Council, that the evacuation of all women, children, the aged and infirm, other than defense workers, within a radius of 20 blocks of Ft. MacArthur was "considered desirable."

Simultaneously a teletype was broadcast by Chief of Police C. B. Horrall directing all police division commanders to assist in the evacuation of women and children, the aged and infirm, other than defense workers, from zones in a one-fourth mile radius of all aircraft manufacturing plants, oil tanks, oil farms and refineries.

Horrall explained that such evacuation was not compulsory, but ordered division commanders to inform all persons designated as living in such zones that they are advised to evacuate if possible. The move is explained as being a precautionary measure and not mandatory.

No alarm should be felt by the residents of the city proper, he said.

"We asked the co-operation of the entire population in remaining away from this restricted area," Col. Hicks said.

No information regarding what will be done with the women and children from the fort was forthcoming. It was intimated that should the evacuation of residents within the 20-block radius from the fort be ordered by Sheriff Biscailuz that it would be up to the County Defense Council to provide for their housing.

Such evacuation would affect an estimated 20,000 persons.

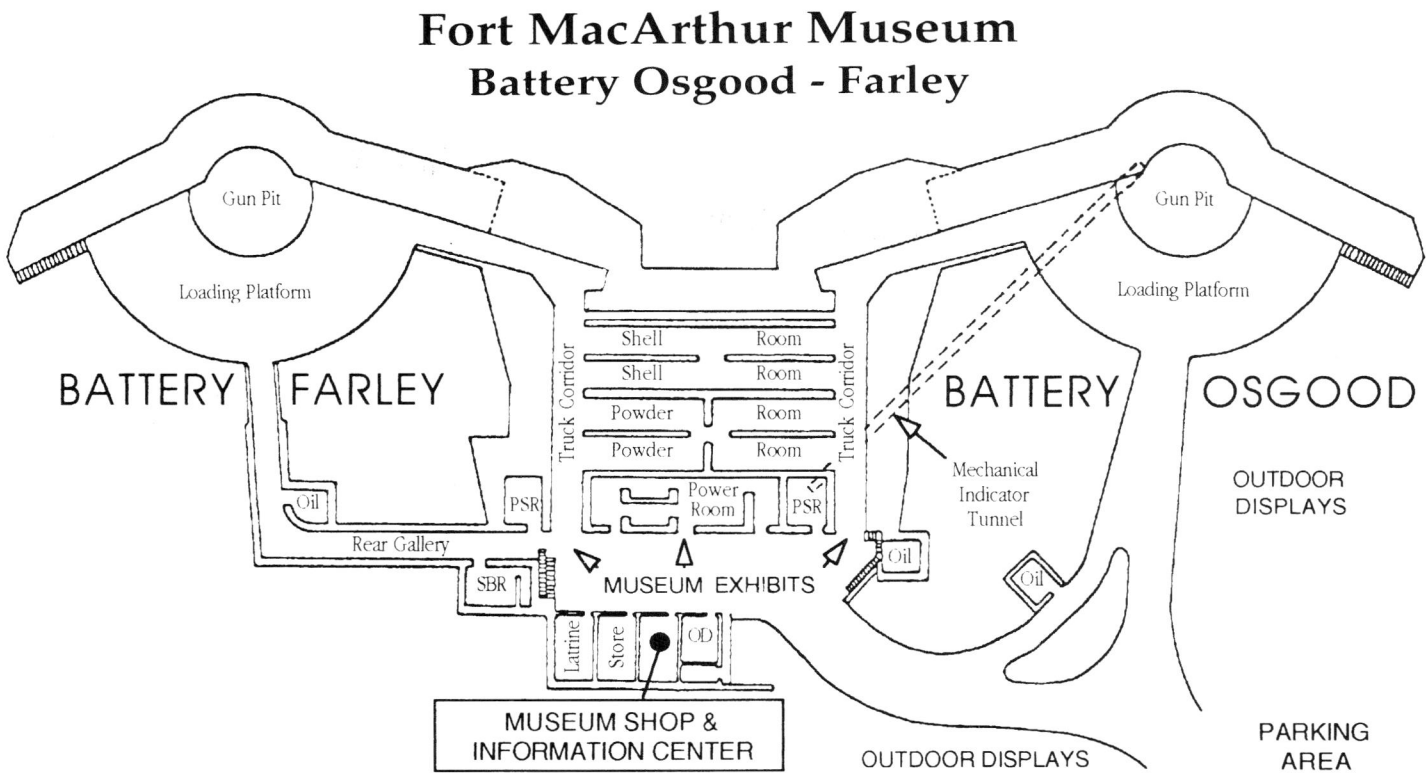

14" rifle on a M1910M1 L.F. Disappearing Carriage, firing from Battery Osgood-Farley, Fort MacArthur. FORT MACARTHUR MUSEUM

THE WEST COAST GOES TO WAR   125

Ft. Stevens State Park
Hammond, Oregon

The Pacific Rim Peace Memorial inscription reads: "Dedicated to members of the 249th Coast Artillery Corps Regiment, Headquarters, Harbor Defense of the Columbia River, and all other United States personnel stationed at Fort Stevens, Fort Clanby, Fort Columbia, and the crew of the Japanese submarine, the *I-25*. Near this place on the night of June 21, 1942, they faced each other when the Japanese submarine shelled Fort Stevens, making it the first foreign attack on a continental military installation since the War of 1812. May peace between the nations be everlasting. Dedicated June 21, 1992." This monument is located at Battery Russell, Fort Stevens State Park. INSET: Shell fragment recovered from the camouflage net that covered Battery Russell.

Coast in Panic, Jap Radio Blares

TOKYO, June 23 (Japanese broadcast recorded by UP, San Francisco)—Tokyo radio said Tuesday that as a result of the shelling of the Oregon coast late Sunday night, residents of the United States from Canada to Mexico "are panic stricken and are leaving in huge numbers for the interior."

JAPS SHELL OREGON SHORE

★

SO... "It Can't Happen Here!"
WELL... IT HAS!

What are YOU doing to SINK the sub that shelled our shores

★ ARE YOU BUYING WAR SAVING STAMPS EVERY DAY?
★ ARE YOU INVESTING 10% OF YOUR SALARY IN WAR SAVINGS BONDS?

Meier & Frank Co.

Sign posted at Fort Stevens by GIs after the shelling.

One of the shell holes from Japanese submarine *I-25*.

This monument is located on Del Laura Beach Road near Fort Stevens State Park.

THE WEST COAST GOES TO WAR

Fujita planned suicide

by Marjorie Woodfin,
Curry Coastal Pilot Correspondent, Brookings, Oregon

There is more to the story of the samurai sword in the Chetco Community Public Library than most Brookings-Harbor residents know.

Most people know that the sword was presented to the city by Nobuo Fujita as an act of apology for fire-bombing the nearby forest during World War II.

Only a few of those responsible for the first visit to the city of Brookings, 20 years after his act of war, by the sword's owner, were aware that he brought the sword, not to present it to the city, but to use it.

His daughter, Yoriko Asakura, was quoted in Fujita's obituary published in the Oct. 3 issue of *The New York Times*, "He thought perhaps people would still be angry and would throw eggs at him. If that happened, he wanted to take responsibility for what he had done."

Asakura said that the planned act of taking responsibility to appease Oregonians if they were still angry at him for the bombing, was to use the sword to commit seppuku, the Japanese traditional ritual suicide, disemboweling himself with the sword.

Fujita was apparently unaware during that first visit, and subsequent visits, of those Brookings residents who were still angry enough with him to place threatening phone calls to those preparing to welcome him to the city.

Instead of using the 400-year-old sword that had accompanied him on the bombing flights to destroy himself, he presented it to the city as a lasting memorial of his sorrow.

Fujita continued to revere his connection with Brookings over the years, and chose to take with him to his cremation, a shirt presented to him by the city during one of his visits.

Former Brookings resident Ernie Bowers delivered the proclamation of friendship from the city and attended the funeral ceremonies.

The family had been notified that the proclamation from the city was on its way, and they told Bowers Fujita was "so excited" when they told him it was coming.

However, Bowers arrived at Fujita's hospital room 20 minutes after his death.

In the hospital room, Bowers discovered a bag with two Brookings T-shirts in the room. The family said Fujita had planned to wear one for his arrival.

Instead, it went with him to his cremation. The family kept the other one as a memorial.

Bowers said the family asked him to return the proclamation to the city to be placed in the case at the library that holds the sword.

Bowers said he promised the family to deliver it personally, and will bring it with him on his next visit from his home in Vancouver.

During his time in Japan after Fujita's death, Bowers participated in several ceremonies, a night vigil at a shrine with family members, and in the cremation and collection of bones.

Family members pick small pieces of bone from the cremated remains, place them in small urns and keep them for memorials of dead loved ones. Bowers was instructed to follow the family custom, using chopsticks to pick up small bone fragments for his own small urn.

Bowers recalled Fujita's excitement following a flight over Mount Emily during his last visit when he was allowed to take control of the aircraft. "He said it was the highlight of his life to fly the plane over Mount Emily," Bowers recalled.

The shared flight of two World War II enemies was perhaps a fitting tribute to the peace Fujita prayed for as he planted the seedling redwood at the bomb site on the 50th anniversary of his war time flight. —October 22, 1997

Top: Chief Flying Officer Nobuo Fujita of Japanese submarine *I-25*. He died on Sept. 30, 1997, at age 86. FORT STEVENS STATE PARK.
Bottom: Nobuo Fujita presents his Samurai sword to Brookings mayor, Tom Davis, at the Chetco Community Public Library on May 27, 1995. The sword was given to the citizens of Brookings in 1962 by Fujita and is now on permanent display in the library. CURRY COASTAL PILOT

World War II Sites to Visit on the West Coast

WASHINGTON
1. Pacific Reserve Fleet at Bremerton
2. Bremerton Naval Museum
3. Puget Sound Naval Shipyard, Bremerton
4. Fort Canby and Fort Columbia state parks, at the mouth of the Columbia River
5. Naval Undersea Museum, Keyport
6. Fort Flagler, Port Townsend
7. Coast Artillery Museum at Fort Worden State Park, Port Townsend
8. Fort Worden State Park, Port Townsend
9. Hanford Engineer Works, Richland
10. Museum of Flight, Seattle
11. Coast Guard Museum, Northwest, Seattle
12. Fort Lawton, Seattle
13. Felts Field, Spokane
14. Fairchild Air Force Base Museum, Spokane
15. Fort George Wright, Spokane
16. Fort Lewis Military Museum, Tacoma
17. McChord Air Museum, Tacoma
18. Puyallup Assembly Center for Ethnic Japanese (Camp Harmony), Puyallup
19. Vancouver Barracks, Vancouver
20. The George C. Marshall House, Vancouver
21. Pearson Air Museum, Vancouver
22. Fort Casey State Park, Couperille
23. Fort Ebey State Park, Whidbey Island

OREGON
1. Columbia River Maritime Museum, Astoria
2. Fort Stevens State Park, Hammond
3. Fort Stevens Museum, Hammond
4. Japanese Balloon Bomb Deaths on Gearhart Mountain Monument, near Bly
5. Fire Bombing Sign, Brookings
6. The Bomber Complex, Milwaukee
7. Oregon Maritime Center and Museum, Portland
8. Oregon Military Museum, Clackamas
9. Naval Air Station Museum, Tillamook

CALIFORNIA
1. General Patton Memorial Museum, Chiriaco Summit
2. Travis Air Force Museum, Travis AFB
3. Japanese-American National Museum, Los Angeles
4. Martyrs Memorial & Museum of the Holocaust, Los Angeles
5. Planes of Fame Air Museum, Chino
6. The Yanks Air Museum, Chino
7. The "Lane Victory" ship, San Pedro
8. Los Angeles Maritime Museum, San Pedro
9. Fort MacArthur Museum, San Pedro
10. *Queen Mary*, Long Beach
11. March Field Museum, Riverside
12. Museum of Flying, Santa Monica
13. Manzanar Relocation Camp, Lone Pine
14. Edward F. Beale Museum, Marysville
15. Castle Air Museum, Merced
16. Flight Test Historical Museum, Edwards AFB
17. U.S. Army Museum, Presidio of Monterey, Monterey
18. CEC/Seabee Museum, Port Hueneme
19. California Citizen Soldier Museum, Sacramento
20. Cabrillo National Monument, San Diego
21. Amphibian Vehicle Museum, San Diego
22. San Diego Aerospace Museum, San Diego
23. U.S. Marines Command Museum, San Diego
24. Fort Funston, San Francisco
25. The Holocaust Center of Northern California, San Francisco
26. Lincoln Park Monuments, San Francisco
27. The "Jeremiah O'Brien" Liberty Ship, San Francisco
28. The Presidio of San Francisco and Museum, San Francisco
29. Fort Point National Historic Site, San Francisco
30. The West Coast Memorial, San Francisco
31. National Maritime Museum and Submarine *Pampanito*, San Francisco
32. San Francisco War Memorial, San Francisco
33. Angel Island and Fort McDowell, San Francisco
34. Lawrence Hall of Science, Berkeley
35. Golden Gate National Recreation Area and Forts Baker, Barry and Cronkite, San Francisco
36. Suisun Bay Mothball Anchorage, Suisun Bay
37. The NASA Ames Research Center, Sunnyvale
38. Treasure Island Museum, San Francisco
39. The Vallejo Naval & Historical Museum, Vallejo
40. The Ellwood Oil Facility, Ellwood
41. Santa Maria Museum of Flight, Santa Maria
42. The Hiller Aviation Museum, San Carlos
43. Tule Lake, Relocation Camp, Tule Lake
44. Emma Wood State Beach, Ventura

For a detailed description of the World War II sites refer to: *World War II Sites in the United States, a Tour Guide & Directory* by Richard E. Osborne, Riebel-Rogue Publishing Co., Indianapolis, Indiana, 1996.

About the Author

Don DeNevi taught courses in psychology at the College of Alameda, in Alameda, Calif., and to inmates serving life sentences at Soledad State Prison, near Salinas, Calif.. He has authored 28 books, including Riddle of the Rock—The Only Successful Escape from Alcatraz. His other volumes range in subjects from California history to space flight, earthquake science, World War II railroad mobilization, and biographies.

DeNevi graduated in 1959 from the University of the Pacific in Stockton, Calif., with a B.A. in history and art. He subsequently earned his Masters and Ed.D. in Education from the University of California at Berkeley. He was affiliated with college teaching for 35 years. In addition to his writing (he has several movie treatments in circulation), he paints watercolors of imaginary, whimsical cities, birds, butterflies, and landscapes.

Other Pictorial Histories Publishing Company books dealing with the early years of World War II:

Artillery at the Golden Gate, the Harbor Defense of San Francisco in World War II.
Destination Tokyo, A Pictorial History of Doolittle's Tokyo Raid, April 18, 1942.
Enemy on Island, Issue in Doubt, the Capture of Wake Island, December 1941.
East Wind Rain, A Pictorial History of the Pearl Harbor Attack.
The Forgotten War, World War II in Alaska & Northwestern Canada, four volumes
A Glorious Page in Our History, The Battle of Midway, 4–6 June 1942.
Prints in the Sand, the U.S. Coast Guard Beach Patrol During World War II.
V for Victory, America's Home Front During World War II.

For a complete catalog write to Pictorial Histories Publishing Company,
713 S. Third Street West, Missoula, MT 59801.
email: phpc@montana.com